Writer's Workshop
• Grade 5 •

Printed on recycled paper.

MACMILLAN/McGRAW-HILL SCHOOL PUBLISHING COMPANY
New York • Chicago • Columbus

ILLUSTRATION CREDITS

Matt Faulkner, 132; Diane La Raya, 128; N. Jo Leonard, 139; Sally
Springer, 130, 131; Jan Pyk, 116; Freya Tanz, 127, 129, 199.

Macmillan/McGraw-Hill School Division
10 Union Square East
New York, New York 10003

Printed in the United States of America

ISBN 0-02-179925-3 / 5

3 4 5 6 7 8 9 POH 99 98 97 96 95 94 93

• MACMILLAN/MCGRAW-HILL •

Writer's Workshop
• Grade 5 •

• HANDBOOK FOR READING/LANGUAGE ARTS TEACHERS •

INTRODUCTION   vi

DAILY LANGUAGE ACTIVITIES AND WEEKLY REVIEW PARAGRAPHS
Overview   2
Language Skills Trace   3
Sentences and Paragraphs   6

GRAMMAR, MECHANICS, AND USAGE HANDBOOK AND GLOSSARY
Overview   79
Punctuation Guide   80
Abbreviations   83
Capitalization Guide   84
Usage Guide   86
Glossary   89
Language Terms   93
Literary Terms   96

WRITING MODELS
Overview   100
Visitor's Guide   101
Speech   102
How-To Guide   103
Personal Narrative   104
Story   105
Limerick   106
Letter   107
Character Sketch   108
Report   109
Book Review   110
Comparison/Contrast Composition   111
Invitation   112
Letter   113
Directions to a Place   114
Form   115
Announcement   116
Scene   117
Biography   118

TABLE OF CONTENTS

WRITING PROMPTS

Overview	120
Visitor's Guide	121
How-To Guide	122
Story	123
Letter	124
Report	125
Comparison/Contrast Composition	126
Story	127
Description	128
Persuasive Letter	129
How-To Guide	130
Comparison/Contrast Composition	131
Comparison/Contrast Composition	132

SPELLING RESOURCES

Overview	134
Spelling Article, Charles Temple	135
How to Study Spelling Words: Chart	139

SPELLING ACTIVITIES
171

SPELLING STRATEGIES AND TIPS
177

Word Finder for Words Most Often Misspelled	182

SPELLING FORMS
185

Student Records	187
Class Records	190

CUMULATIVE WORD LIST
193

HANDWRITING RESOURCES

Overview	198
Handwriting Reminders	199
Handwriting Guidelines	200

HANDWRITING MODELS
203

The **Writer's Workshop: Handbook for Reading/Language Arts Teachers** presents exercises and activities in a concrete, easy-to-use format. It is designed to strengthen student reading and writing skills on a continual basis.

In the **Daily Language Activities** section, students can review punctuation, capitalization, and usage skills in a proofreading context. There are activities, three sentences a day, for thirty-six weeks of work; at the end of each week, there is a review paragraph containing all the spelling errors from the selection-related spelling lists in the unit.

The **Grammar, Mechanics, and Usage Handbook and Glossary** includes comprehensive and accessible information on punctuation and capitalization, as well as usage of nouns, verbs, and adjectives. The Glossary contains definitions for writing, language, and literary terms. You may wish to duplicate this Handbook and Glossary for your students and ask them to keep it in their writing folder for easy reference.

The **Models for Self-Evaluation** are provided so that students can compare written examples generated in the writing process in each unit to a well-developed, annotated model to see how their finished writing compares. The models cover a wide variety of genres. Writing Prompts and Picture Prompts are presented to motivate student writing in response to a variety of verbal and visual cues.

The **Spelling Resources** section provides more than five hundred semantically patterned sentences to enhance students' comprehension of selected words. Through the use of pretests and posttests, students can self-correct their work and analyze their errors. They may also participate in generalized spelling activities provided for practicing spelling; these include general spelling rules and a list of words most often misspelled on each grade level.

The **Spelling Resources** section also includes individual and class record forms, a Personal Spelling List which may be duplicated, and an indispensable Spelling Strategies and Tips unit.

The **Handwriting Resources** present handwriting reminders and a student self-check guide along with handwriting guidelines. This list of handwriting reminders is intended as an aid for students as they check their work for legibility.

DAILY LANGUAGE ACTIVITIES

Daily Language Activities and Weekly Review Paragraphs

Overview of the Section

The purpose of the daily language activities and weekly review paragraphs contained in this section of the **Writer's Workshop** is to review punctuation, capitalization, and usage skills in a proofreading context.

There are activities, three sentences per day, for thirty-six weeks of work. At the end of each week, there is a review paragraph containing all the skills covered during the week. In addition, this paragraph contains five spelling errors from the selection-related spelling lists in the unit. The week's sentences and review paragraphs are both related to the theme of the unit.

Format of the Activities and Paragraphs

The daily sentences are set up in two columns. In the left column are the sentences to be corrected. In the right column are the corrected sentences. The first review paragraph on the page is the paragraph to be corrected. The second paragraph is the corrected paragraph.

Using the Activities and Paragraphs

You may elect to write the incorrect sentences on the chalkboard each day and ask students to correct them orally. Or you may wish to make transparencies from these materials, which would be particularly effective for the review paragraphs.

How you decide to present the activities and paragraphs is, of course, your choice. However, they have been designed as quick, five- to ten-minute daily proofreading activities, which are most effective when making the corrections as they go along.

The **Grammar, Mechanics, and Usage Handbook** on page 79 provides rules and examples for the skills contained in the daily activities. Students can refer to this **Handbook** as needed.

Skills Included in the Activities and Paragraphs

For your information, the skills covered in these activities are presented in a matrix on the following page.

Unit Theme: Unforgettable Places

Unit/Week	Language Skill	Spelling Words Tested in Review Paragraphs
Unit 1, Week 1	Capitalization and punctuation of declarative and imperative sentences	border final fail wise sailor
Unit 1, Week 2	Capitalization and punctuation of declarative, imperative, and interrogative sentences	narrow evening jewel temper scold
Unit 1, Week 3	Capitalization and punctuation of declarative and exclamatory sentences; and after interjections	pleasure delicious adventure cushion manage
Unit 1, Week 4	Capitalization and punctuation in compound sentences	ancient palace furnace enormous explore
Unit 1, Week 5	Review of punctuation for four sentence types	border evening ancient pleasure explore
Unit 1, Week 6	Review of punctuation for compound sentences	England Spain Japan France Russia

Unit Theme: Transformations

Unit/Week	Language Skill	Spelling Words Tested in Review Paragraphs
Unit 2, Week 7	Capitalization of names and titles	location government arch architect apartment
Unit 2, Week 8	Capitalization and punctuation of dates	expect fortune invention creative information
Unit 2, Week 9	Capitalization and punctuation of places and addresses	instant distant cupboard pale guilt
Unit 2, Week 10	Capitalization and punctuation of abbreviations and initials	opposite performance powerful celebrate celebration
Unit 2, Week 11	Review of capitalization and punctuation of names, titles, and dates	information instant architect opposite celebrate
Unit 2, Week 12	Review of capitalization and punctuation of places, abbreviations, and initials	New York Pennsylvania Connecticut New Jersey Delaware

Unit Theme: Against the Odds

Unit/Week	Language Skill	Spelling Words Tested in Review Paragraphs
Unit 3, Week 13	Subject-verb agreement	contest champion include figure trophy
Unit 3, Week 14	Troublesome verb pairs; verb usage	impossible guard possibility project ache
Unit 3, Week 15	Punctuation of contractions	treatment emergency pressure suppose amazing
Unit 3, Week 16	Verb usage	medical suggestion medicine attention direction
Unit 3, Week 17	Review of subject-verb agreement and verb usage	contest possibility champion amazing attention
Unit 3, Week 18	Review of punctuation of contractions and verb usage	Vermont Maine New Hampshire Rhode Island Massachusetts

Unit Theme: Getting to Know You

Unit/Week	Language Skill	Spelling Words Tested in Review Paragraphs
Unit 4, Week 19	Pronoun usage	raspberry watermelon cantaloupe discuss scarf
Unit 4, Week 20	Pronoun/verb agreement; pronoun/antecedent agreement	novel terrified editor appearance terrific
Unit 4, Week 21	Punctuation of possessive nouns	bare collar splendid beggar church
Unit 4, Week 22	Punctuation of verb contractions; and contractions with pronouns	banquet Caribbean festival favorite sunset
Unit 4, Week 23	Review of pronoun usage	splendid novel Caribbean editor discuss
Unit 4, Week 24	Review of punctuation in contractions and possessive nouns	Iowa Michigan Indiana Illinois Arkansas

Unit Theme: Way to Go

Unit/Week	Language Skill	Spelling Words Tested in Review Paragraphs
Unit 5, Week 25	Adjective/adverb usage	applause motorcycle comparison dozen quarter
Unit 5, Week 26	Adjective usage	alert careful cautious skillful quiver
Unit 5, Week 27	Adjective/adverb usage	rifle tremble pistol groan moan
Unit 5, Week 28	Punctuation of words in a series	anxious survive endure frantically surrender
Unit 5, Week 29	Review of adjective/adverb usage	pistol endure survive tremble quiver
Unit 5, Week 30	Review of adjective/adverb usage	Georgia Florida Alabama Kansas Nebraska

Unit Theme: Are You Sure?

Unit/Week	Language Skill	Spelling Words Tested in Review Paragraphs
Unit 6, Week 31	Capitalization and punctuation of quotations	experiment assignment scientist investigate accurate
Unit 6, Week 32	Capitalization and punctuation of quotations	dinosaur museum skeleton restore display
Unit 6, Week 33	Capitalization and punctuation of titles of works	puzzle mystery puzzling committee mysterious
Unit 6, Week 34	Words often confused—homophones	invade monster invasion argue bawl
Unit 6, Week 35	Review of capitalization and punctuation of quotations	mystery museum skeleton puzzle puzzling
Unit 6, Week 36	Review of capitalization and punctuation of titles and words often confused	Nevada Utah Montana Oregon Wyoming

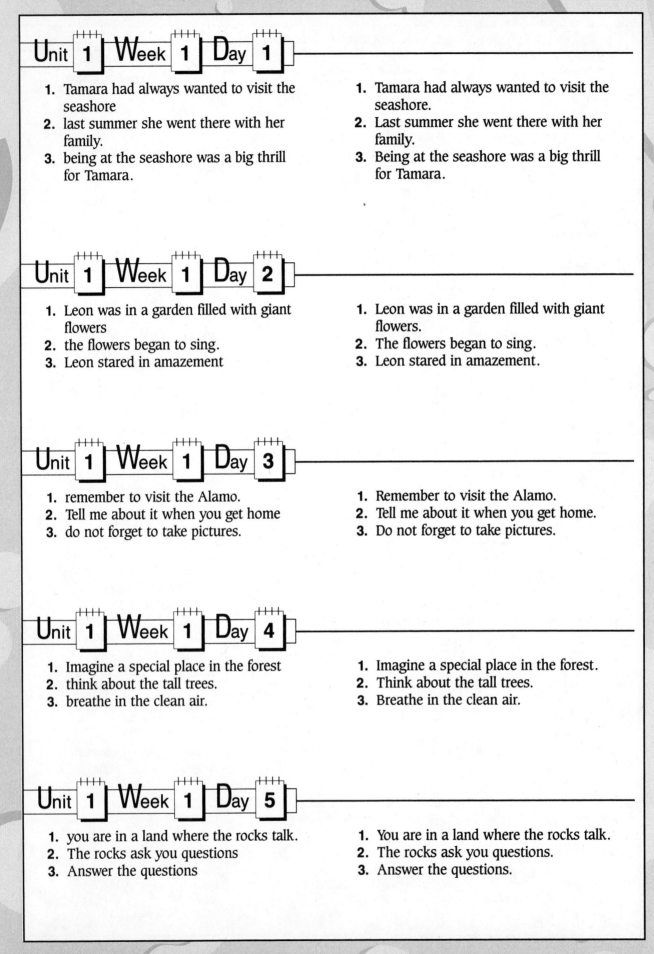

Unit 1 | Week 1 | Day 1

1. Tamara had always wanted to visit the seashore
2. last summer she went there with her family.
3. being at the seashore was a big thrill for Tamara.

1. Tamara had always wanted to visit the seashore.
2. Last summer she went there with her family.
3. Being at the seashore was a big thrill for Tamara.

Unit 1 | Week 1 | Day 2

1. Leon was in a garden filled with giant flowers
2. the flowers began to sing.
3. Leon stared in amazement

1. Leon was in a garden filled with giant flowers.
2. The flowers began to sing.
3. Leon stared in amazement.

Unit 1 | Week 1 | Day 3

1. remember to visit the Alamo.
2. Tell me about it when you get home
3. do not forget to take pictures.

1. Remember to visit the Alamo.
2. Tell me about it when you get home.
3. Do not forget to take pictures.

Unit 1 | Week 1 | Day 4

1. Imagine a special place in the forest
2. think about the tall trees.
3. breathe in the clean air.

1. Imagine a special place in the forest.
2. Think about the tall trees.
3. Breathe in the clean air.

Unit 1 | Week 1 | Day 5

1. you are in a land where the rocks talk.
2. The rocks ask you questions
3. Answer the questions

1. You are in a land where the rocks talk.
2. The rocks ask you questions.
3. Answer the questions.

REVIEW PARAGRAPH FOR PROOFREADING

Ten-year-old Trish stepped off the ship that carried her to this mysterious island. she looked at the boarder of beach that separated the sea from the mountains beyond. Trish did not think she would like it here She felt a tingle go up her spine Suddenly, Trish remembered the finel words of a wyse sailer. "Do not be afraid You will get used to your new home. you will not fale."

Ten-year-old Trish stepped off the ship that carried her to this mysterious island. She looked at the border of beach that separated the sea from the mountains beyond. Trish did not think she would like it here. She felt a tingle go up her spine. Suddenly, Trish remembered the final words of a wise sailor. "Do not be afraid. You will get used to your new home. You will not fail."

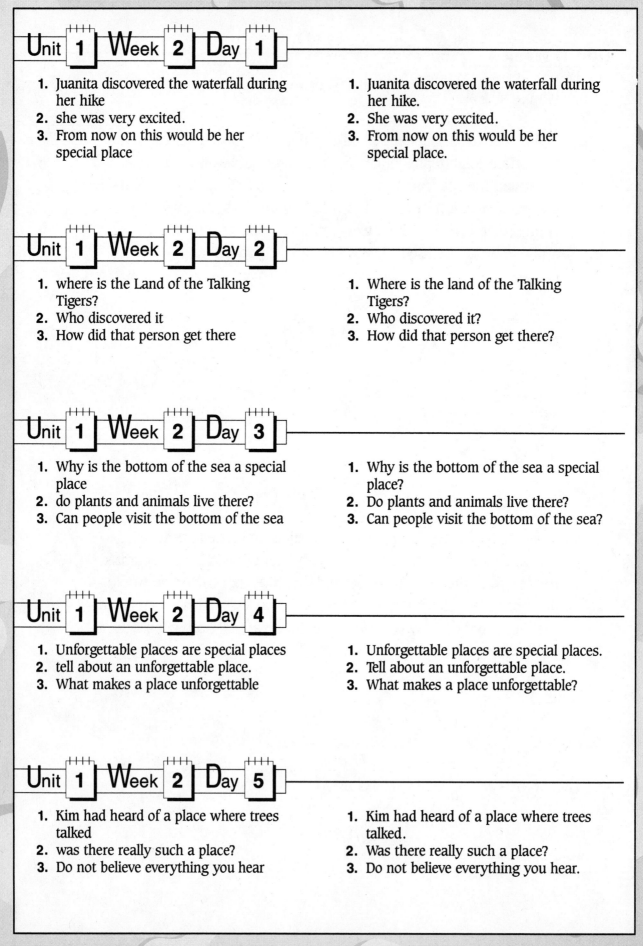

Unit 1 Week 2 Day 1

1. Juanita discovered the waterfall during her hike
2. she was very excited.
3. From now on this would be her special place

1. Juanita discovered the waterfall during her hike.
2. She was very excited.
3. From now on this would be her special place.

Unit 1 Week 2 Day 2

1. where is the Land of the Talking Tigers?
2. Who discovered it
3. How did that person get there

1. Where is the land of the Talking Tigers?
2. Who discovered it?
3. How did that person get there?

Unit 1 Week 2 Day 3

1. Why is the bottom of the sea a special place
2. do plants and animals live there?
3. Can people visit the bottom of the sea

1. Why is the bottom of the sea a special place?
2. Do plants and animals live there?
3. Can people visit the bottom of the sea?

Unit 1 Week 2 Day 4

1. Unforgettable places are special places
2. tell about an unforgettable place.
3. What makes a place unforgettable

1. Unforgettable places are special places.
2. Tell about an unforgettable place.
3. What makes a place unforgettable?

Unit 1 Week 2 Day 5

1. Kim had heard of a place where trees talked
2. was there really such a place?
3. Do not believe everything you hear

1. Kim had heard of a place where trees talked.
2. Was there really such a place?
3. Do not believe everything you hear.

REVIEW PARAGRAPHS FOR PROOFREADING

One evning Peter took a walk along the narow path in the forest As he leaned down to look at a sparkling red juel on the ground, he saw a person jump out from behind a tree. "You shouldn't jump out like that," Peter shouted. "You scared me. tell me who you are and what you want."

"How dare you skold me," said the handsome stranger. "Do not fear me I am the Guardian of the Forest. Do you like stories Would you like to hear a story about the forest?"

Peter nodded and sat down. the stranger sat down beside him and began his story. As Peter listened, he forgot his bad tempur and was no longer afraid.

One evening Peter took a walk along the narrow path in the forest. As he leaned down to look at a sparkling red jewel on the ground, he saw a person jump out from behind a tree. "You shouldn't jump out like that," Peter shouted. "You scared me. Tell me who you are and what you want."

"How dare you scold me," said the handsome stranger. "Do not fear me. I am the Guardian of the Forest. Do you like stories? Would you like to hear a story about the forest?"

Peter nodded and sat down. The stranger sat down beside him and began his story. As Peter listened, he forgot his bad temper and was no longer afraid.

Unit 1 | Week 3 | Day 1

1. that is the most beautiful mountain I have ever seen
2. I can't wait to get to the top
3. what a special place!

1. That is the most beautiful mountain I have ever seen.
2. I can't wait to get to the top!
3. What a special place!

Unit 1 | Week 3 | Day 2

1. this museum is unforgettable!
2. I am so glad we came here
3. I have never seen a building so large

1. This museum is unforgettable!
2. I am so glad we came here!
3. I have never seen a building so large!

Unit 1 | Week 3 | Day 3

1. Hooray Here we are at Disney World!
2. Wow! this is a great place
3. Whew Disney World sure is crowded!

1. Hooray! Here we are at Disney World!
2. Wow! This is a great place!
3. Whew! Disney World sure is crowded!

Unit 1 | Week 3 | Day 4

1. Wow I'll never forget the beauty of these woods!
2. Gosh It is so peaceful here
3. oh! there goes a deer!

1. Wow! I'll never forget the beauty of these woods!
2. Gosh! It is so peaceful here!
3. Oh! There goes a deer!

Unit 1 | Week 3 | Day 5

1. There's a horse flying in the sky
2. it can't be true.
3. This is an unusual place

1. There's a horse flying in the sky!
2. It can't be true.
3. This is an unusual place.

REVIEW PARAGRAPH FOR PROOFREADING

We walked and walked along the mountain trail We walked for what seemed like forever Ouch My feet never hurt like this before I couldn't manige another step! my troop leader said that this would be an advenchure and that I would have fun. fun! All I wanted was a soft cushen to rest on and the plezure of eating some delisious food

---

We walked and walked along the mountain trail. We walked for what seemed like forever. Ouch! My feet never hurt like this before! I couldn't manage another step! My troop leader said that this would be an adventure and that I would have fun. Fun! All I wanted was a soft cushion to rest on and the pleasure of eating some delicious food.

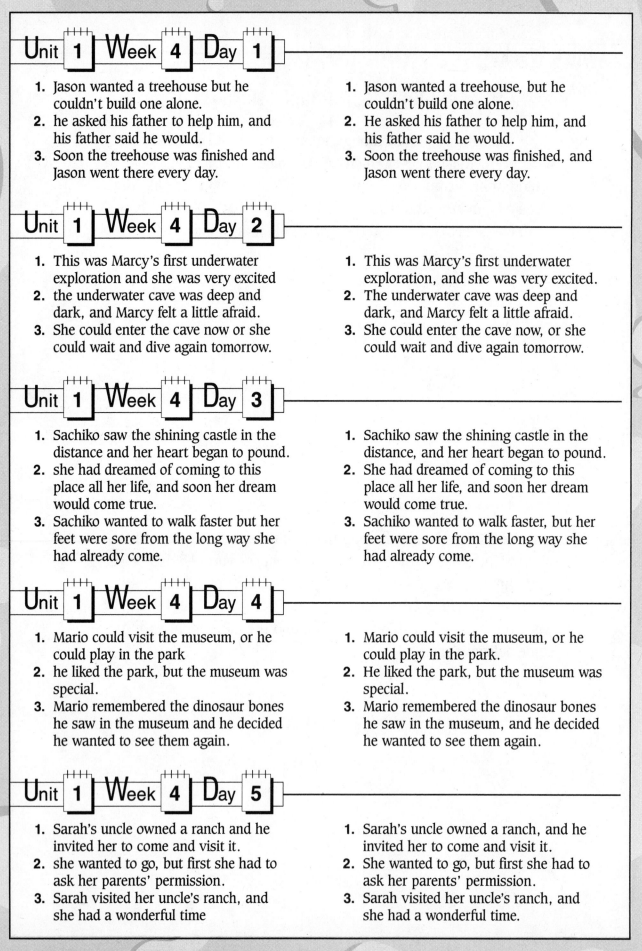

Unit 1 | Week 4 | Day 1

1. Jason wanted a treehouse but he couldn't build one alone.
2. he asked his father to help him, and his father said he would.
3. Soon the treehouse was finished and Jason went there every day.

1. Jason wanted a treehouse, but he couldn't build one alone.
2. He asked his father to help him, and his father said he would.
3. Soon the treehouse was finished, and Jason went there every day.

Unit 1 | Week 4 | Day 2

1. This was Marcy's first underwater exploration and she was very excited
2. the underwater cave was deep and dark, and Marcy felt a little afraid.
3. She could enter the cave now or she could wait and dive again tomorrow.

1. This was Marcy's first underwater exploration, and she was very excited.
2. The underwater cave was deep and dark, and Marcy felt a little afraid.
3. She could enter the cave now, or she could wait and dive again tomorrow.

Unit 1 | Week 4 | Day 3

1. Sachiko saw the shining castle in the distance and her heart began to pound.
2. she had dreamed of coming to this place all her life, and soon her dream would come true.
3. Sachiko wanted to walk faster but her feet were sore from the long way she had already come.

1. Sachiko saw the shining castle in the distance, and her heart began to pound.
2. She had dreamed of coming to this place all her life, and soon her dream would come true.
3. Sachiko wanted to walk faster, but her feet were sore from the long way she had already come.

Unit 1 | Week 4 | Day 4

1. Mario could visit the museum, or he could play in the park
2. he liked the park, but the museum was special.
3. Mario remembered the dinosaur bones he saw in the museum and he decided he wanted to see them again.

1. Mario could visit the museum, or he could play in the park.
2. He liked the park, but the museum was special.
3. Mario remembered the dinosaur bones he saw in the museum, and he decided he wanted to see them again.

Unit 1 | Week 4 | Day 5

1. Sarah's uncle owned a ranch and he invited her to come and visit it.
2. she wanted to go, but first she had to ask her parents' permission.
3. Sarah visited her uncle's ranch, and she had a wonderful time

1. Sarah's uncle owned a ranch, and he invited her to come and visit it.
2. She wanted to go, but first she had to ask her parents' permission.
3. Sarah visited her uncle's ranch, and she had a wonderful time.

REVIEW PARAGRAPHS FOR PROOFREADING

The anshunt palase was enormus and Brian was determined to exploar every room. he hoped he would find some wonderful treasure.

Brian entered the first room The room had no furniture but in one corner stood a firnace. It was covered in bright yellow and white jewels. "Treasure! I found treasure!" Brian shouted. "Should I run home now to tell everyone about it or should I look for more?" Brian wondered

Brian decided to look for more but he didn't find anything else. still, Brian was a happy boy who enjoyed a wonderful adventure.

The ancient palace was enormous, and Brian was determined to explore every room. He hoped he would find some wonderful treasure.

Brian entered the first room. The room had no furniture, but in one corner stood a furnace. It was covered in bright yellow and white jewels. "Treasure! I found treasure!" Brian shouted. "Should I run home now to tell everyone about it, or should I look for more?" Brian wondered.

Brian decided to look for more, but he didn't find anything else. Still, Brian was a happy boy who enjoyed a wonderful adventure.

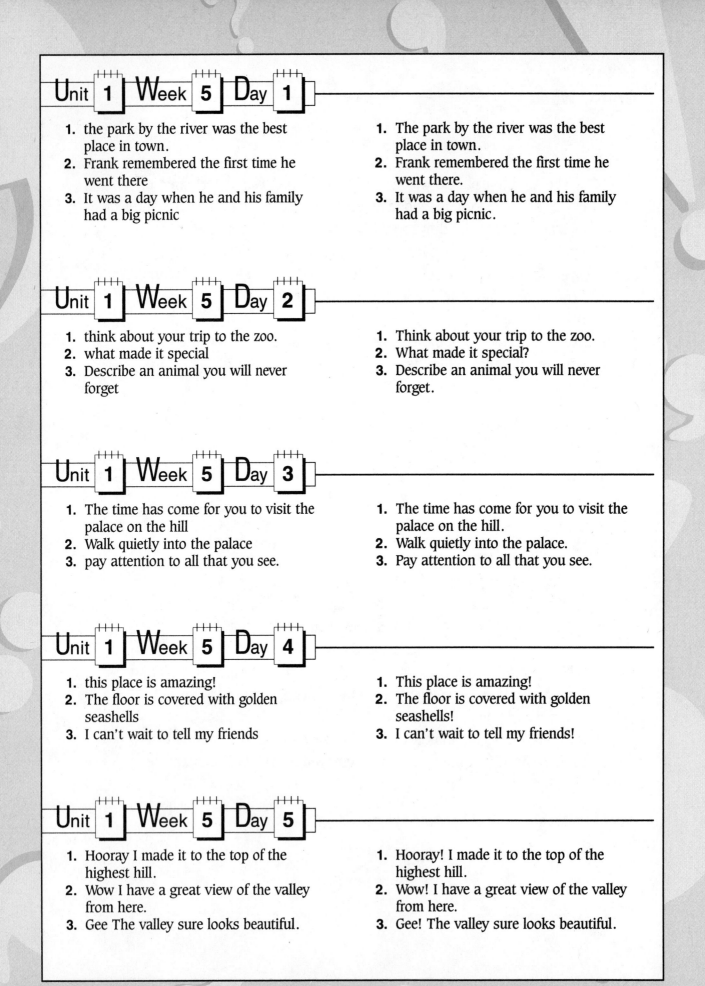

Unit 1 Week 5 Day 1

1. the park by the river was the best place in town.
2. Frank remembered the first time he went there
3. It was a day when he and his family had a big picnic

1. The park by the river was the best place in town.
2. Frank remembered the first time he went there.
3. It was a day when he and his family had a big picnic.

Unit 1 Week 5 Day 2

1. think about your trip to the zoo.
2. what made it special
3. Describe an animal you will never forget

1. Think about your trip to the zoo.
2. What made it special?
3. Describe an animal you will never forget.

Unit 1 Week 5 Day 3

1. The time has come for you to visit the palace on the hill
2. Walk quietly into the palace
3. pay attention to all that you see.

1. The time has come for you to visit the palace on the hill.
2. Walk quietly into the palace.
3. Pay attention to all that you see.

Unit 1 Week 5 Day 4

1. this place is amazing!
2. The floor is covered with golden seashells
3. I can't wait to tell my friends

1. This place is amazing!
2. The floor is covered with golden seashells!
3. I can't wait to tell my friends!

Unit 1 Week 5 Day 5

1. Hooray I made it to the top of the highest hill.
2. Wow I have a great view of the valley from here.
3. Gee The valley sure looks beautiful.

1. Hooray! I made it to the top of the highest hill.
2. Wow! I have a great view of the valley from here.
3. Gee! The valley sure looks beautiful.

Review Paragraphs for Proofreading

Early one evenning Joan decided to explour the woods and she came upon an ancient castle. when Joan knocked on the castle door, a young girl answered. She invited Joan to come inside, and the two talked for a while Then the young girl said, "Do you like dolls I hope so. come and look at my collection of doll's clothing."

All of the clothing was lovely but one dress was special. Along the bourder of the neck was the finest lace Joan had ever seen. She said, "Wow This lace is beautiful Do you know how to make it I would love to learn."

"It would be a plesure to teach you," the girl replied

Joan smiled. she knew she had made a new friend.

Early one evening Joan decided to explore the woods, and she came upon an ancient castle. When Joan knocked on the castle door, a young girl answered. She invited Joan to come inside, and the two talked for a while. Then the young girl said, "Do you like dolls? I hope so. Come and look at my collection of doll's clothing."

All of the clothing was lovely, but one dress was special. Along the border of the neck was the finest lace Joan had ever seen. She said, "Wow! This lace is beautiful! Do you know how to make it? I would love to learn."

"It would be a pleasure to teach you," the girl replied.

Joan smiled. She knew she had made a new friend.

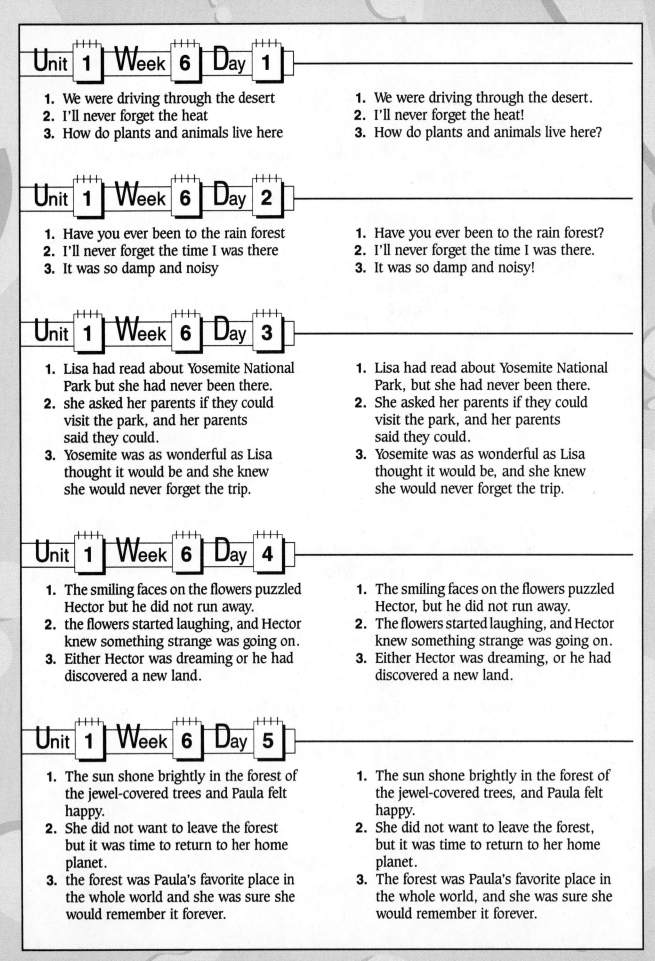

Unit 1 Week 6 Day 1

1. We were driving through the desert
2. I'll never forget the heat
3. How do plants and animals live here

1. We were driving through the desert.
2. I'll never forget the heat!
3. How do plants and animals live here?

Unit 1 Week 6 Day 2

1. Have you ever been to the rain forest
2. I'll never forget the time I was there
3. It was so damp and noisy

1. Have you ever been to the rain forest?
2. I'll never forget the time I was there.
3. It was so damp and noisy!

Unit 1 Week 6 Day 3

1. Lisa had read about Yosemite National Park but she had never been there.
2. she asked her parents if they could visit the park, and her parents said they could.
3. Yosemite was as wonderful as Lisa thought it would be and she knew she would never forget the trip.

1. Lisa had read about Yosemite National Park, but she had never been there.
2. She asked her parents if they could visit the park, and her parents said they could.
3. Yosemite was as wonderful as Lisa thought it would be, and she knew she would never forget the trip.

Unit 1 Week 6 Day 4

1. The smiling faces on the flowers puzzled Hector but he did not run away.
2. the flowers started laughing, and Hector knew something strange was going on.
3. Either Hector was dreaming or he had discovered a new land.

1. The smiling faces on the flowers puzzled Hector, but he did not run away.
2. The flowers started laughing, and Hector knew something strange was going on.
3. Either Hector was dreaming, or he had discovered a new land.

Unit 1 Week 6 Day 5

1. The sun shone brightly in the forest of the jewel-covered trees and Paula felt happy.
2. She did not want to leave the forest but it was time to return to her home planet.
3. the forest was Paula's favorite place in the whole world and she was sure she would remember it forever.

1. The sun shone brightly in the forest of the jewel-covered trees, and Paula felt happy.
2. She did not want to leave the forest, but it was time to return to her home planet.
3. The forest was Paula's favorite place in the whole world, and she was sure she would remember it forever.

REVIEW PARAGRAPH FOR PROOFREADING

The plane touched down on the runway and I woke up. I was home from my vacation. What a great time I had I did not have the chance to visit Englund, Spian, or Franse but I did spend a lot of time in Jappan and Russa. Who could ever forget the sights in Kyoto Who would not enjoy seeing Moscow? I may never get back to these places, but I don't care. They will live forever in my memory Don't miss a chance to visit these faraway lands.

The plane touched down on the runway, and I woke up. I was home from my vacation. What a great time I had! I did not have the chance to visit England, Spain, or France, but I did spend a lot of time in Japan and Russia. Who could ever forget the sights in Kyoto? Who would not enjoy seeing Moscow? I may never get back to these places, but I don't care. They will live forever in my memory. Don't miss a chance to visit these faraway lands.

Unit 2 | Week 7 | Day 1

1. Over time, betty changed from being shy to being friendly.
2. Now, laura wanted to be her friend.
3. The new boy in school, peter, wanted to be her friend, too.

1. Over time, Betty changed from being shy to being friendly.
2. Now, Laura wanted to be her friend.
3. The new boy in school, Peter, wanted to be her friend, too.

Unit 2 | Week 7 | Day 2

1. The science teacher explained to michael how a tadpole becomes a frog.
2. He was fascinated and told his little sister cynthia.
3. She decided to ask joanne about tadpoles and frogs.

1. The science teacher explained to Michael how a tadpole becomes a frog.
2. He was fascinated and told his little sister Cynthia.
3. She decided to ask Joanne about tadpoles and frogs.

Unit 2 | Week 7 | Day 3

1. In May uncle john went on a diet to lose weight.
2. He asked aunt ann to go on a diet with him, and she did.
3. When grandma rosa came to visit in the winter, aunt ann and uncle john looked very different.

1. In May, Uncle John went on a diet to lose weight.
2. He asked Aunt Ann to go on a diet with him, and she did.
3. When Grandma Rosa came to visit in the winter, Aunt Ann and Uncle John looked very different.

Unit 2 | Week 7 | Day 4

1. Before he entered politics, president ronald reagan was an actor.
2. After studying to become a teacher, coach jones became a baseball player instead.
3. My friend doctor warren once worked as a carpenter.

1. Before he entered politics, President Ronald Reagan was an actor.
2. After studying to become a teacher, Coach Jones became a baseball player instead.
3. My friend Doctor Warren once worked as a carpenter.

Unit 2 | Week 7 | Day 5

1. Usually doctor ruiz is a calm person, but today he was very excited.
2. I spoke to nurse walker about the change.
3. She told me that tomorrow the doctor would receive an important award from mayor Jenkins.

1. Usually Doctor Ruiz is a calm person, but today he was very excited.
2. I spoke to Nurse Walker about the change.
3. She told me that tomorrow the doctor would receive an important award from Mayor Jenkins.

REVIEW PARAGRAPHS FOR PROOFREADING

On Monday Uncle Henry went to see Mayor amanda riles. Uncle Henry was an arkitect who designed tall buildings, especially apartmunt houses and goverment buildings. At their meeting, mayor Riles asked Uncle Henry if he would like to design a new building for city workers. She explained that she wanted a building that would change the look of the city. She said she wanted a building with a tall, wide artch, but that the locashun of the building had not been decided yet.

After talking a little longer, uncle Henry told the Mayor that he would design the building. The two shook hands, and Uncle henry left happy because he had an exciting new project!

On Monday, Uncle Henry went to see Mayor Amanda Riles. Uncle Henry was an architect who designed tall buildings, especially apartment houses and government buildings. At their meeting, Mayor Riles asked Uncle Henry if he would like to design a new building for city workers. She explained that she wanted a building that would change the look of the city. She said she wanted a building with a tall, wide arch, but that the location of the building had not been decided yet.

After talking a little longer, Uncle Henry told the mayor that he would design the building. The two shook hands, and Uncle Henry left happy because he had an exciting new project!

Unit 2 Week 8 Day 1

1. On monday the buds on the rosebush were tightly closed.
2. On wednesday the buds were beginning to open.
3. By friday all of the roses on the bush were in full bloom.

1. On Monday, the buds on the rosebush were tightly closed.
2. On Wednesday, the buds were beginning to open.
3. By Friday, all of the roses on the bush were in full bloom.

Unit 2 Week 8 Day 2

1. Even people who are not normally friendly laugh and smile at christmas.
2. During easter my family takes plain white eggs and decorates them to look like jewels.
3. On independence day we celebrate the day on which the American colonies became a free country.

1. Even people who are not normally friendly laugh and smile at Christmas.
2. During Easter, my family takes plain white eggs and decorates them to look like jewels.
3. On Independence Day, we celebrate the day on which the American colonies became a free country.

Unit 2 Week 8 Day 3

1. By the end of september the air has changed from being warm to being cool.
2. In april the colorless garden becomes filled with the reds and yellows of spring flowers.
3. Every january the snow falls and makes the trees look like they are covered with fine white lace.

1. By the end of September, the air has changed from being warm to being cool.
2. In April, the colorless garden becomes filled with the reds and yellows of spring flowers.
3. Every January, the snow falls and makes the trees look like they are covered with fine white lace.

Unit 2 Week 8 Day 4

1. The name of my club changed on Friday, June 28 1991.
2. On Monday, july 8, we met in a new place.
3. Starting thursday, August 1, we met once a week instead of twice.

1. The name of my club changed on Friday, June 28, 1991.
2. On Monday, July 8, we met in a new place.
3. Starting Thursday, August 1, we met once a week instead of twice.

Unit 2 Week 8 Day 5

1. Thomas Alva Edison was born on Thursday, February 11 1847.
2. on tuesday, October 21, 1879, Edison invented the electric light bulb and changed people's lives forever.
3. Thomas Alva Edison died on Sunday, october 18, 1931.

1. Thomas Alva Edison was born on Thursday, February 11, 1847.
2. On Tuesday, October 21, 1879, Edison invented the electric light bulb and changed people's lives forever.
3. Thomas Alva Edison died on Sunday, October 18, 1931.

REVIEW PARAGRAPHS FOR PROOFREADING

One of the world's most famous and kreative inventors was born on wednesday march 3 1847. His name was Alexander Graham Bell, and on tuesday march 7 1876, he received a patent for inventing the telephone. In 1880 the country of France gave Bell a reward of ten thousand dollars for his invenshun. In those days that amount of money was a foretune.

The telephone changed the way people lived. Infourmation that once took days, weeks, or even longer to get from one place to another now took only minutes. However, as time went on, people came to ekspect their messages to travel even faster. Today, special fiber-optic cables make it possible to send messages in seconds!

One of the world's most famous and creative inventors was born on Wednesday, March 3, 1847. His name was Alexander Graham Bell, and on Tuesday, March 7, 1876, he received a patent for inventing the telephone. In 1880, the country of France gave Bell a reward of ten thousand dollars for his invention. In those days that amount of money was a fortune.

The telephone changed the way people lived. Information that once took days, weeks, or even longer to get from one place to another now took only minutes. However, as time went on, people came to expect their messages to travel even faster. Today, special fiber-optic cables make it possible to send messages in seconds!

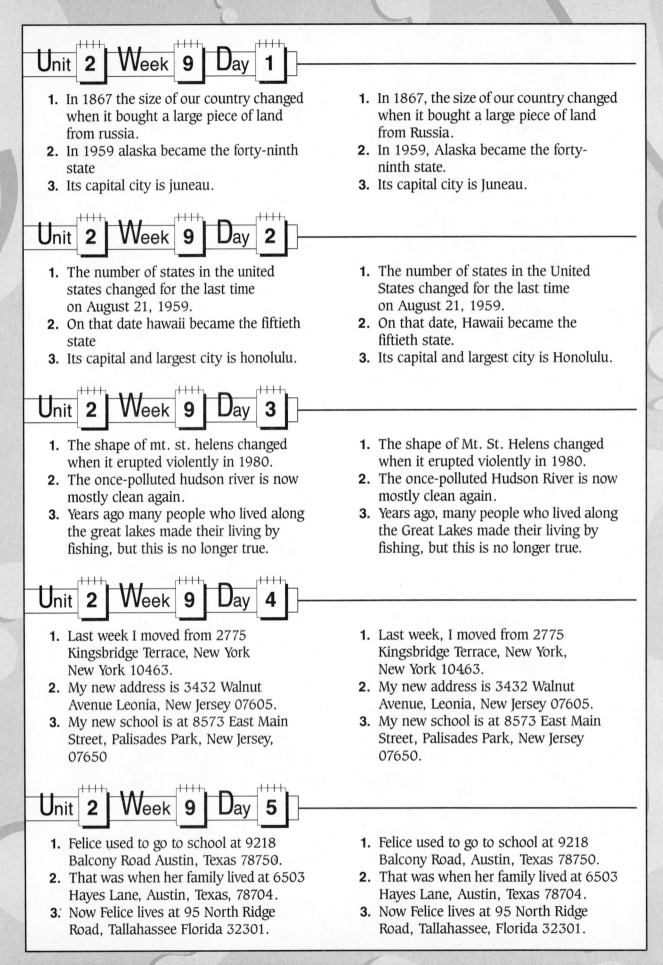

Unit 2 | Week 9 | Day 1

1. In 1867 the size of our country changed when it bought a large piece of land from russia.
2. In 1959 alaska became the forty-ninth state
3. Its capital city is juneau.

1. In 1867, the size of our country changed when it bought a large piece of land from Russia.
2. In 1959, Alaska became the forty-ninth state.
3. Its capital city is Juneau.

Unit 2 | Week 9 | Day 2

1. The number of states in the united states changed for the last time on August 21, 1959.
2. On that date hawaii became the fiftieth state
3. Its capital and largest city is honolulu.

1. The number of states in the United States changed for the last time on August 21, 1959.
2. On that date, Hawaii became the fiftieth state.
3. Its capital and largest city is Honolulu.

Unit 2 | Week 9 | Day 3

1. The shape of mt. st. helens changed when it erupted violently in 1980.
2. The once-polluted hudson river is now mostly clean again.
3. Years ago many people who lived along the great lakes made their living by fishing, but this is no longer true.

1. The shape of Mt. St. Helens changed when it erupted violently in 1980.
2. The once-polluted Hudson River is now mostly clean again.
3. Years ago, many people who lived along the Great Lakes made their living by fishing, but this is no longer true.

Unit 2 | Week 9 | Day 4

1. Last week I moved from 2775 Kingsbridge Terrace, New York New York 10463.
2. My new address is 3432 Walnut Avenue Leonia, New Jersey 07605.
3. My new school is at 8573 East Main Street, Palisades Park, New Jersey, 07650

1. Last week, I moved from 2775 Kingsbridge Terrace, New York, New York 10463.
2. My new address is 3432 Walnut Avenue, Leonia, New Jersey 07605.
3. My new school is at 8573 East Main Street, Palisades Park, New Jersey 07650.

Unit 2 | Week 9 | Day 5

1. Felice used to go to school at 9218 Balcony Road Austin, Texas 78750.
2. That was when her family lived at 6503 Hayes Lane, Austin, Texas, 78704.
3. Now Felice lives at 95 North Ridge Road, Tallahassee Florida 32301.

1. Felice used to go to school at 9218 Balcony Road, Austin, Texas 78750.
2. That was when her family lived at 6503 Hayes Lane, Austin, Texas 78704.
3. Now Felice lives at 95 North Ridge Road, Tallahassee, Florida 32301.

REVIEW PARAGRAPHS FOR PROOFREADING

Kate picked up the letter that rested on the cupbored and stared at the envelope. The address on it was 2356 Grace Drive Port Richey, florida 34668. This was Kate's new home.

In an instint Kate's memory wandered back to last year when she lived on the other side of the united states. At that time her address was 6093 Wallace Street, seattle, Washington, 98102. Her life had changed so much between then and now. Before when she looked out her window, she saw distint mount rainier. Now when she looked outside, she saw the gulf of mexico.

Kate became pail as she felt an attack of gilt for the hard time she had given her parents over the move.

Kate picked up the letter that rested on the cupboard and stared at the envelope. The address on it was 2356 Grace Drive, Port Richey, Florida 34668. This was Kate's new home.

In an instant, Kate's memory wandered back to last year when she lived on the other side of the United States. At that time, her address was 6093 Wallace Street, Seattle, Washington 98102. Her life had changed so much between then and now. Before, when she looked out her window, she saw distant Mount Rainier. Now, when she looked outside, she saw the Gulf of Mexico.

Kate became pale as she felt an attack of guilt for the hard time she had given her parents over the move.

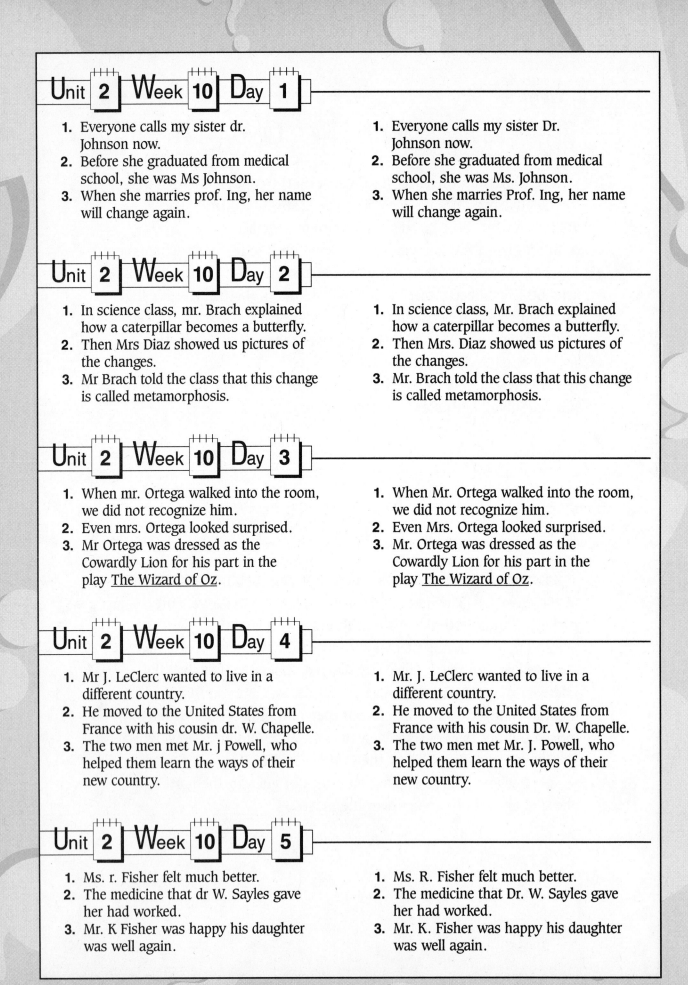

Unit 2 | Week 10 | Day 1

1. Everyone calls my sister dr. Johnson now.
2. Before she graduated from medical school, she was Ms Johnson.
3. When she marries prof. Ing, her name will change again.

1. Everyone calls my sister Dr. Johnson now.
2. Before she graduated from medical school, she was Ms. Johnson.
3. When she marries Prof. Ing, her name will change again.

Unit 2 | Week 10 | Day 2

1. In science class, mr. Brach explained how a caterpillar becomes a butterfly.
2. Then Mrs Diaz showed us pictures of the changes.
3. Mr Brach told the class that this change is called metamorphosis.

1. In science class, Mr. Brach explained how a caterpillar becomes a butterfly.
2. Then Mrs. Diaz showed us pictures of the changes.
3. Mr. Brach told the class that this change is called metamorphosis.

Unit 2 | Week 10 | Day 3

1. When mr. Ortega walked into the room, we did not recognize him.
2. Even mrs. Ortega looked surprised.
3. Mr Ortega was dressed as the Cowardly Lion for his part in the play The Wizard of Oz.

1. When Mr. Ortega walked into the room, we did not recognize him.
2. Even Mrs. Ortega looked surprised.
3. Mr. Ortega was dressed as the Cowardly Lion for his part in the play The Wizard of Oz.

Unit 2 | Week 10 | Day 4

1. Mr J. LeClerc wanted to live in a different country.
2. He moved to the United States from France with his cousin dr. W. Chapelle.
3. The two men met Mr. j Powell, who helped them learn the ways of their new country.

1. Mr. J. LeClerc wanted to live in a different country.
2. He moved to the United States from France with his cousin Dr. W. Chapelle.
3. The two men met Mr. J. Powell, who helped them learn the ways of their new country.

Unit 2 | Week 10 | Day 5

1. Ms. r. Fisher felt much better.
2. The medicine that dr W. Sayles gave her had worked.
3. Mr. K Fisher was happy his daughter was well again.

1. Ms. R. Fisher felt much better.
2. The medicine that Dr. W. Sayles gave her had worked.
3. Mr. K. Fisher was happy his daughter was well again.

REVIEW PARAGRAPHS FOR PROOFREADING

The town was divided into two groups of people who had oposite ideas about how to selebrate Independence Day. One group was

lead by mr. g. Walsh, and the other group was lead by Mrs. S Winter. Mr. Walsh wanted to have a town picnic. Mrs Winter wanted to stage a performance of the signing of the Declaration of Independence. For weeks, neither leader would give in to the other.

Then one day Mr. Walsh went to see dr. b Pauly, who was a very pouerful person in the town. Dr. Pauly persuaded Mr Walsh to go along with mrs. Winter, and the town had a wonderful celabration on the Fourth of July.

The town was divided into two groups of people who had opposite ideas about how to celebrate Independence Day. One group was led by Mr. G. Walsh, and the other group was led by Mrs. S. Winter. Mr. Walsh wanted to have a town picnic. Mrs. Winter wanted to stage a performance of the signing of the Declaration of Independence. For weeks, neither leader would give in to the other.

Then one day Mr. Walsh went to see Dr. B. Pauly, who was a very powerful person in the town. Dr. Pauly persuaded Mr. Walsh to go along with Mrs. Winter, and the town had a wonderful celebration on the Fourth of July.

Unit 2 | Week 11 | Day 1

1. My sister wanda told a story about a king who had a magic touch.
2. The king's name was midas, and all that he touched turned to gold.
3. The Greek god dionysius laughed when all the food Midas ate turned to gold in his mouth.

1. My sister Wanda told a story about a king who had a magic touch.
2. The king's name was Midas, and all that he touched turned to gold.
3. The Greek god Dionysius laughed when all the food Midas ate turned to gold in his mouth.

Unit 2 | Week 11 | Day 2

1. In July uncle robert finished painting the house a different color.
2. He asked aunt miranda if she liked the new color of the house.
3. She told him that she did and that grandfather ross liked it, too.

1. In July, Uncle Robert finished painting the house a different color.
2. He asked Aunt Miranda if she liked the new color of the house.
3. She told him that she did and that Grandfather Ross liked it, too.

Unit 2 | Week 11 | Day 3

1. Before she became a teacher, professor minton was an artist.
2. Donald wants to change jobs and become a basketball coach like coach white.
3. The town used to have three doctors, but now there is only doctor marshall.

1. Before she became a teacher, Professor Minton was an artist.
2. Donald wants to change jobs and become a basketball coach like Coach White.
3. The town used to have three doctors, but now there is only Doctor Marshall.

Unit 2 | Week 11 | Day 4

1. On saturday, Marissa walked into the school auditorium and could not believe her eyes.
2. It was the same auditorium she had been in on friday, but overnight it had been transformed into a pirate's cove.
3. Then she remembered it was may, the month of the big school play.

1. On Saturday, Marissa walked into the school auditorium and could not believe her eyes.
2. It was the same auditorium she had been in on Friday, but overnight it had been transformed into a pirate's cove.
3. Then she remembered it was May, the month of the big school play.

Unit 2 | Week 11 | Day 5

1. Soviet astronaut Yuri Gagarin was born on March 9 1934.
2. On April 12 1961 Gagarin changed the course of history when he became the first person to travel into space.
3. Yuri Gagarin died on March 27 1968 near Moscow.

1. Soviet astronaut Yuri Gagarin was born on March 9, 1934.
2. On April 12, 1961, Gagarin changed the course of history when he became the first person to travel into space.
3. Yuri Gagarin died on March 27, 1968, near Moscow.

REVIEW PARAGRAPHS FOR PROOFREADING

On monday may 18 1992 the new bridge connecting Marble Island to Hackettstown was opened to traffic. The architekt of the bridge, maya lang, was at the opening festivities, and so was Mayor sonia hernandez, the mayor of Hackettstown. In addition, about three hundred citizens gathered to celibrate this event that would change their way of life.

At noon, mayor Hernandez spoke and reviewed informasion about how the bridge was built and how much it cost. Then the Mayor cut a ribbon at the Marble Island entrance to the bridge. In that instunt cars started to drive to the oppossite side of the bridge and into Hackettstown.

On Monday, May 18, 1992, the new bridge connecting Marble Island to Hackettstown was opened to traffic. The architect of the bridge, Maya Lang, was at the opening festivities, and so was Mayor Sonia Hernandez, the mayor of Hackettstown. In addition, about three hundred citizens gathered to celebrate this event that would change their way of life.

At noon, Mayor Hernandez spoke and reviewed information about how the bridge was built and how much it cost. Then the mayor cut a ribbon at the Marble Island entrance to the bridge. In that instant, cars started to drive to the opposite side of the bridge and into Hackettstown.

1. The city of san francisco was once a small settlement.
2. When gold was discovered on the american river in 1848, the population of the city grew and grew.
3. Today the city is the third largest in california.

1. The city of San Francisco was once a small settlement.
2. When gold was discovered on the American River in 1848, the population of the city grew and grew.
3. Today the city is the third largest in California.

1. The ancient city of the Incas is called machu picchu.
2. The city is in the andes mountains.
3. Today the city is one of the most popular tourist attractions in south america.

1. The ancient city of the Incas is called Machu Picchu.
2. The city is in the Andes Mountains.
3. Today the city is one of the most popular tourist attractions in South America.

1. Last week Dan moved from 1243 Barker Road Mt. Pleasant, Iowa 52641.
2. He now lives at 144-20 Simpson Street, Flushing New York 11355.
3. He will go to school at 221-02 Northern Boulevard, Bayside, New York, 11361.

1. Last week, Dan moved from 1243 Barker Road, Mt. Pleasant, Iowa 52641.
2. He now lives at 144-20 Simpson Street, Flushing, New York 11355.
3. He will go to school at 221-02 Northern Boulevard, Bayside, New York 11361.

1. Mr. t. Franklin began to jog every day.
2. His friend dr K. Walton said it would be good for his health.
3. After four weeks Mrs N Franklin saw that her husband had more energy than ever before.

1. Mr. T. Franklin began to jog every day.
2. His friend Dr. K. Walton said it would be good for his health.
3. After four weeks, Mrs. N. Franklin saw that her husband had more energy than ever before.

1. On Sunday ms. G. Wong felt fine, but on Monday she felt sick.
2. She went to see Dr D Driscoll, and he gave her medicine.
3. In two days Mrs y Zhin noticed that her niece was better.

1. On Sunday, Ms. G. Wong felt fine, but on Monday, she felt sick.
2. She went to see Dr. D. Driscoll, and he gave her medicine.
3. In two days, Mrs. Y. Zhin noticed that her niece was better.

REVIEW PARAGRAPHS FOR PROOFREADING

Over the years the look of cities in pensylvania, New Jersy, Deleware, conneticut, and New Yorck changed. For example, once the main cities in these states did not have tall buildings. Today, however, places such as pittsburgh, trenton, dover, and hartford all have their steel-and-glass towers.

Perhaps the city best known for its tall buildings is new york city. In 1902 the company of D H Burnham designed the Flatiron Building, the city's first skyscraper. In 1930 mr. W van Alen designed the beautiful 1,048-foot-high Chrysler Building. Mr. p. Johnson and Mr Mies van der Rohe designed the Seagram Building in 1958. Over time more of the towering giants followed, changing the face of the city forever.

Over the years, the look of cities in Pennsylvania, New Jersey, Delaware, Connecticut, and New York changed. For example, once the main cities in these states did not have tall buildings. Today, however, places such as Pittsburgh, Trenton, Dover, and Hartford all have their steel-and-glass towers.

Perhaps the city best known for its tall buildings is New York City. In 1902, the company of D. H. Burnham designed the Flatiron Building, the city's first skyscraper. In 1930, Mr. W. van Alen designed the beautiful 1,048-foot-high Chrysler Building. Mr. P. Johnson and Mr. Mies van der Rohe designed the Seagram Building in 1958. Over time, more of the towering giants followed, changing the face of the city forever.

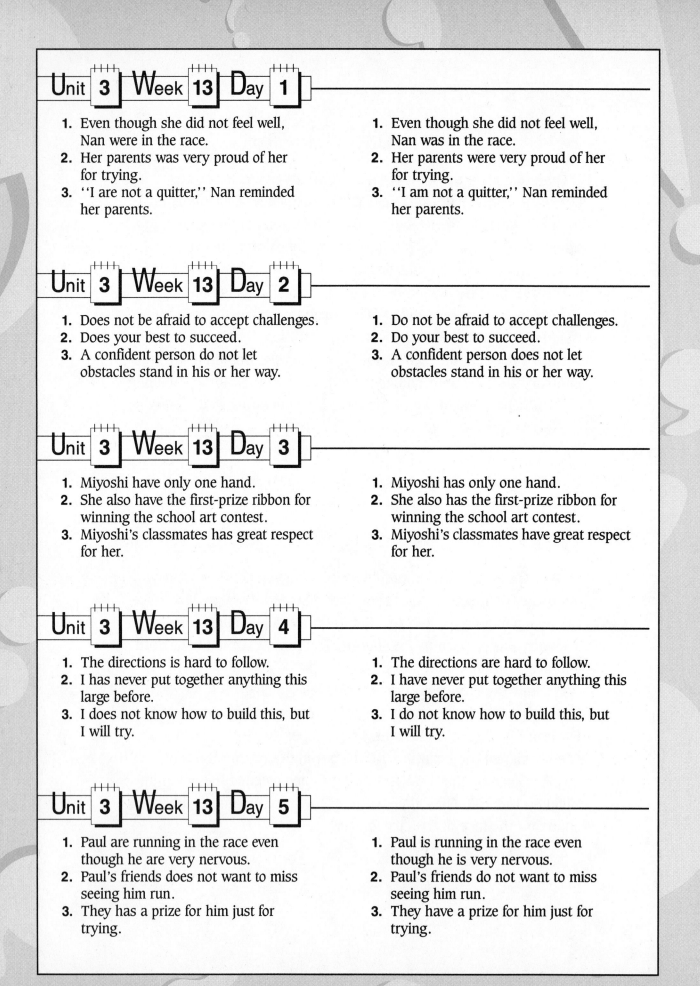

Unit 3 | Week 13 | Day 1

1. Even though she did not feel well, Nan were in the race.
2. Her parents was very proud of her for trying.
3. "I are not a quitter," Nan reminded her parents.

1. Even though she did not feel well, Nan was in the race.
2. Her parents were very proud of her for trying.
3. "I am not a quitter," Nan reminded her parents.

Unit 3 | Week 13 | Day 2

1. Does not be afraid to accept challenges.
2. Does your best to succeed.
3. A confident person do not let obstacles stand in his or her way.

1. Do not be afraid to accept challenges.
2. Do your best to succeed.
3. A confident person does not let obstacles stand in his or her way.

Unit 3 | Week 13 | Day 3

1. Miyoshi have only one hand.
2. She also have the first-prize ribbon for winning the school art contest.
3. Miyoshi's classmates has great respect for her.

1. Miyoshi has only one hand.
2. She also has the first-prize ribbon for winning the school art contest.
3. Miyoshi's classmates have great respect for her.

Unit 3 | Week 13 | Day 4

1. The directions is hard to follow.
2. I has never put together anything this large before.
3. I does not know how to build this, but I will try.

1. The directions are hard to follow.
2. I have never put together anything this large before.
3. I do not know how to build this, but I will try.

Unit 3 | Week 13 | Day 5

1. Paul are running in the race even though he are very nervous.
2. Paul's friends does not want to miss seeing him run.
3. They has a prize for him just for trying.

1. Paul is running in the race even though he is very nervous.
2. Paul's friends do not want to miss seeing him run.
3. They have a prize for him just for trying.

Review Paragraphs for Proofreading

Donna are nervous as she looks at all the faces in the audience. She do not think she can skate in front of all these people. Can she possibly become the ice-skating champeon of her state? Suddenly, Donna hears her name announced over the loudspeakers, and she skates onto the ice. The ice is smooth, and the lights is bright. Donna calms down as she skates one figyure after another. The rest of her routine have to enclude at least two really hard movements, but Donna is not worried.

Soon the kontest are over, and Donna have won. As she steps up to receive her trofy, Donna smiles widely. She have never felt so proud!

Donna is nervous as she looks at all the faces in the audience. She does not think she can skate in front of all these people. Can she possibly become the ice-skating champion of her state? Suddenly, Donna hears her name announced over the loudspeakers, and she skates onto the ice. The ice is smooth, and the lights are bright. Donna calms down as she skates one figure after another. The rest of her routine has to include at least two really hard movements, but Donna is not worried.

Soon the contest is over, and Donna has won. As she steps up to receive her trophy, Donna smiles widely. She has never felt so proud!

Unit 3 | Week 14 | Day 1

1. They have went the distance.
2. They has done a courageous thing.
3. Was you aware of their courage?

1. They have gone the distance.
2. They have done a courageous thing.
3. Were you aware of their courage?

Unit 3 | Week 14 | Day 2

1. Rosa Parks would not set in the back of the bus.
2. She set in the front.
3. Ms. Parks showed courage by setting in the front of the bus.

1. Rosa Parks would not sit in the back of the bus.
2. She sat in the front.
3. Ms. Parks showed courage by sitting in the front of the bus.

Unit 3 | Week 14 | Day 3

1. They was the winners.
2. No one thought they was going to win.
3. How does they keep trying?

1. They were the winners.
2. No one thought they were going to win.
3. How do they keep trying?

Unit 3 | Week 14 | Day 4

1. One of the girls were there.
2. She swum like a champion.
3. I have never saw anyone swim as well.

1. One of the girls was there.
2. She swam like a champion.
3. I have never seen anyone swim as well.

Unit 3 | Week 14 | Day 5

1. Who would have thinked she would win.
2. She brung her whole family to the game.
3. I was so happy when I see her win.

1. Who would have thought she would win.
2. She brought her whole family to the game.
3. I was so happy when I saw her win.

Review Paragraph for Proofreading

Despite a tremendous acke in her leg, Angela has went ahead with her plans to enter the marathon. Angela don't give up easily. She don't think anything is imposible. Completing the marathon is a distinct possability for someone with such a positive attitude. She's always on her garde against negative feelings. Has you ever seen anyone like her? I don't think there's any projuct she can't handle.

Despite a tremendous ache in her leg, Angela has gone ahead with her plans to enter the marathon. Angela doesn't give up easily. She doesn't think anything is impossible. Completing the marathon is a distinct possibility for someone with such a positive attitude. She's always on her guard against negative feelings. Have you ever seen anyone like her? I don't think there's any project she can't handle.

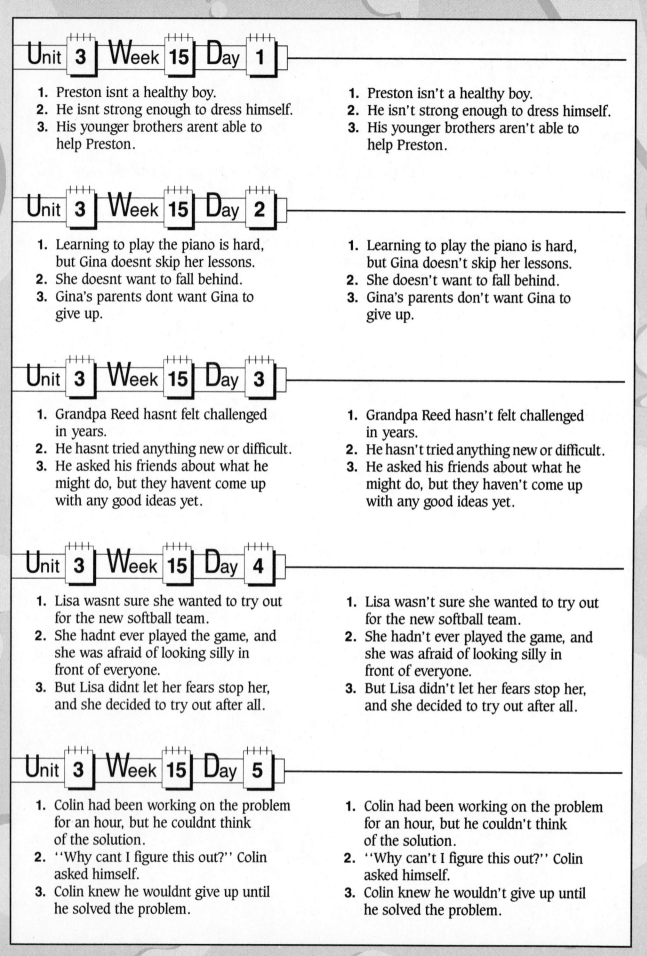

Unit 3 | Week 15 | Day 1

1. Preston isnt a healthy boy.
2. He isnt strong enough to dress himself.
3. His younger brothers arent able to help Preston.

1. Preston isn't a healthy boy.
2. He isn't strong enough to dress himself.
3. His younger brothers aren't able to help Preston.

Unit 3 | Week 15 | Day 2

1. Learning to play the piano is hard, but Gina doesnt skip her lessons.
2. She doesnt want to fall behind.
3. Gina's parents dont want Gina to give up.

1. Learning to play the piano is hard, but Gina doesn't skip her lessons.
2. She doesn't want to fall behind.
3. Gina's parents don't want Gina to give up.

Unit 3 | Week 15 | Day 3

1. Grandpa Reed hasnt felt challenged in years.
2. He hasnt tried anything new or difficult.
3. He asked his friends about what he might do, but they havent come up with any good ideas yet.

1. Grandpa Reed hasn't felt challenged in years.
2. He hasn't tried anything new or difficult.
3. He asked his friends about what he might do, but they haven't come up with any good ideas yet.

Unit 3 | Week 15 | Day 4

1. Lisa wasnt sure she wanted to try out for the new softball team.
2. She hadnt ever played the game, and she was afraid of looking silly in front of everyone.
3. But Lisa didnt let her fears stop her, and she decided to try out after all.

1. Lisa wasn't sure she wanted to try out for the new softball team.
2. She hadn't ever played the game, and she was afraid of looking silly in front of everyone.
3. But Lisa didn't let her fears stop her, and she decided to try out after all.

Unit 3 | Week 15 | Day 5

1. Colin had been working on the problem for an hour, but he couldnt think of the solution.
2. ''Why cant I figure this out?'' Colin asked himself.
3. Colin knew he wouldnt give up until he solved the problem.

1. Colin had been working on the problem for an hour, but he couldn't think of the solution.
2. ''Why can't I figure this out?'' Colin asked himself.
3. Colin knew he wouldn't give up until he solved the problem.

REVIEW PARAGRAPHS FOR PROOFREADING

As soon as Dr. Baylor saw the child's arm, she knew she had an emerjency. She had to stop the bleeding immediately. There wasnt a moment to lose. At first, Dr. Baylor applied presure to the wound, but that didnt work. Next she tied a tourniquet around the child's arm, and soon the bleeding stopped.

''In all my years as a doctor, I havent had a patient as brave as you,'' Doctor Baylor said to the child. ''I supose you are the bravest girl in the whole world.'' In truth, the doctor couldnt believe how amayzing the little girl was. She hadnt cried one tear during the whole treetment. Somehow she had overcome her fear.

As soon as Dr. Baylor saw the child's arm, she knew she had an emergency. She had to stop the bleeding immediately. There wasn't a moment to lose. At first, Dr. Baylor applied pressure to the wound, but that didn't work. Next, she tied a tourniquet around the child's arm, and soon the bleeding stopped.

''In all my years as a doctor, I haven't had a patient as brave as you,'' Doctor Baylor said to the child. ''I suppose you are the bravest girl in the whole world.'' In truth, the doctor couldn't believe how amazing the little girl was. She hadn't cried one tear during the whole treatment. Somehow she had overcome her fear.

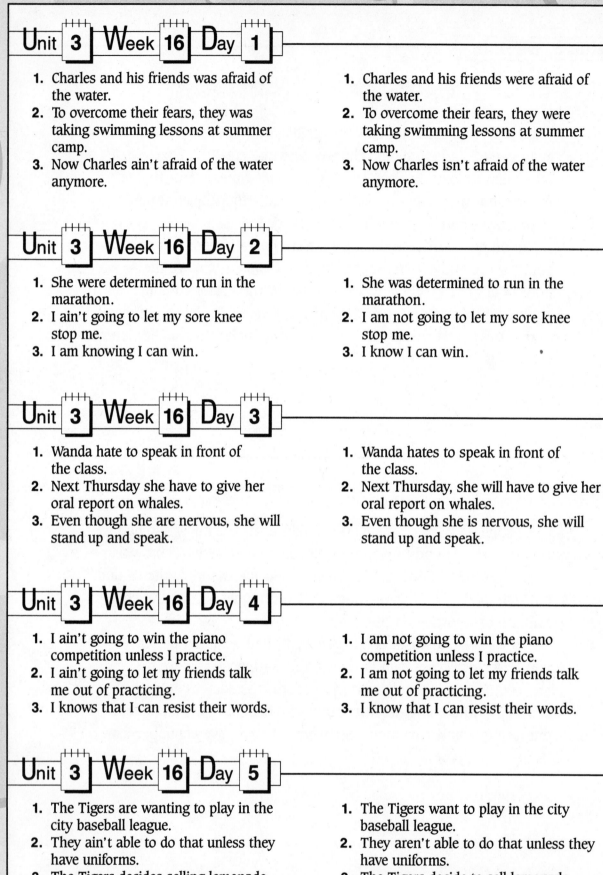

Unit 3 Week 16 Day 1

1. Charles and his friends was afraid of the water.
2. To overcome their fears, they was taking swimming lessons at summer camp.
3. Now Charles ain't afraid of the water anymore.

1. Charles and his friends were afraid of the water.
2. To overcome their fears, they were taking swimming lessons at summer camp.
3. Now Charles isn't afraid of the water anymore.

Unit 3 Week 16 Day 2

1. She were determined to run in the marathon.
2. I ain't going to let my sore knee stop me.
3. I am knowing I can win.

1. She was determined to run in the marathon.
2. I am not going to let my sore knee stop me.
3. I know I can win.

Unit 3 Week 16 Day 3

1. Wanda hate to speak in front of the class.
2. Next Thursday she have to give her oral report on whales.
3. Even though she are nervous, she will stand up and speak.

1. Wanda hates to speak in front of the class.
2. Next Thursday, she will have to give her oral report on whales.
3. Even though she is nervous, she will stand up and speak.

Unit 3 Week 16 Day 4

1. I ain't going to win the piano competition unless I practice.
2. I ain't going to let my friends talk me out of practicing.
3. I knows that I can resist their words.

1. I am not going to win the piano competition unless I practice.
2. I am not going to let my friends talk me out of practicing.
3. I know that I can resist their words.

Unit 3 Week 16 Day 5

1. The Tigers are wanting to play in the city baseball league.
2. They ain't able to do that unless they have uniforms.
3. The Tigers decides selling lemonade in order to raise money for uniforms.

1. The Tigers want to play in the city baseball league.
2. They aren't able to do that unless they have uniforms.
3. The Tigers decide to sell lemonade in order to raise money for uniforms.

REVIEW PARAGRAPHS FOR PROOFREADING

It was on a Sunday afternoon that Pedro sees the bird with the broken wing. He picks it up gently, and take it into the house. ''I wonder if this little one make it?'' Pedro thinks.

Pedro asks his father, a medicle doctor, for a sugestion on how to help the bird. ''I ain't a specialist in bird medcine,'' Pedro's father replies, ''but let's sees what we can do.''

Pedro and his dad put the bird in a shoe box and feed it worms and water. They pays a lot of attenshion to the bird. After a week, the bird am beginning to flap its wings, and Pedro takes it outside and frees it. The bird flew away in the direktion of the sun. ''You made it, little one, you made it.''

It is on a Sunday afternoon that Pedro sees the bird with the broken wing. He picks it up gently, and takes it into the house. ''I wonder if this little one will make it?'' Pedro thinks.

Pedro asks his father, a medical doctor, for a suggestion on how to help the bird. ''I am not a specialist in bird medicine,'' Pedro's father replies, ''but let's see what we can do.''

Pedro and his dad put the bird in a shoe box and feed it worms and water. They pay a lot of attention to the bird. After a week, the bird begins to flap its wings, and Pedro takes it outside and frees it. The bird flies away in the direction of the sun. ''You made it, little one, you made it.''

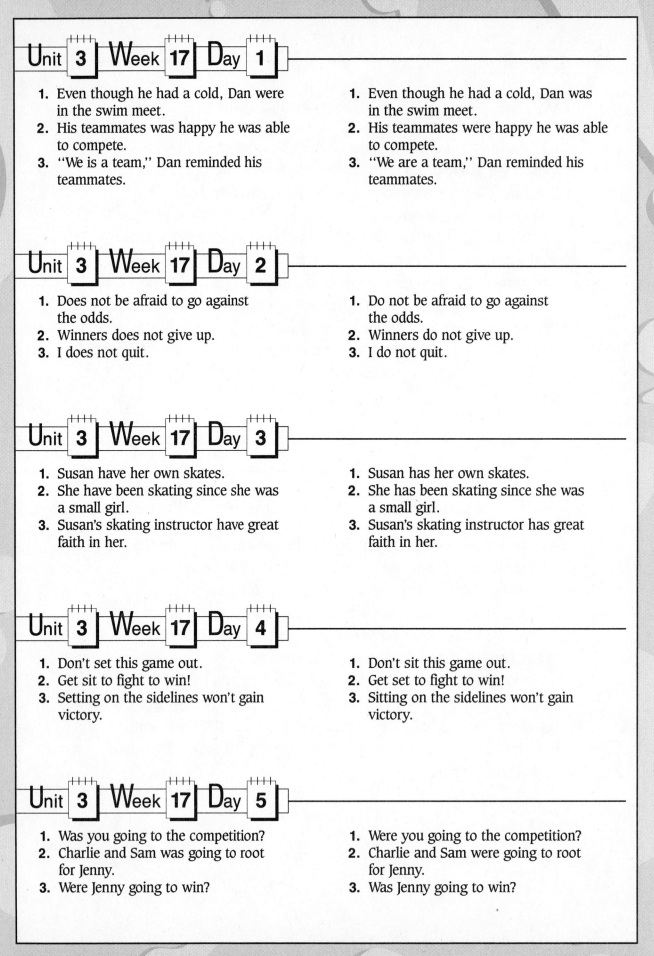

Unit 3 Week 17 Day 1

1. Even though he had a cold, Dan were in the swim meet.
2. His teammates was happy he was able to compete.
3. "We is a team," Dan reminded his teammates.

1. Even though he had a cold, Dan was in the swim meet.
2. His teammates were happy he was able to compete.
3. "We are a team," Dan reminded his teammates.

Unit 3 Week 17 Day 2

1. Does not be afraid to go against the odds.
2. Winners does not give up.
3. I does not quit.

1. Do not be afraid to go against the odds.
2. Winners do not give up.
3. I do not quit.

Unit 3 Week 17 Day 3

1. Susan have her own skates.
2. She have been skating since she was a small girl.
3. Susan's skating instructor have great faith in her.

1. Susan has her own skates.
2. She has been skating since she was a small girl.
3. Susan's skating instructor has great faith in her.

Unit 3 Week 17 Day 4

1. Don't set this game out.
2. Get sit to fight to win!
3. Setting on the sidelines won't gain victory.

1. Don't sit this game out.
2. Get set to fight to win!
3. Sitting on the sidelines won't gain victory.

Unit 3 Week 17 Day 5

1. Was you going to the competition?
2. Charlie and Sam was going to root for Jenny.
3. Were Jenny going to win?

1. Were you going to the competition?
2. Charlie and Sam were going to root for Jenny.
3. Was Jenny going to win?

REVIEW PARAGRAPH FOR PROOFREADING

Jean and Laura was determined to enter the diving conntest. Even though the reigning champian, Patricia Loomis, said they has no possability of winning against her. It's amazeing how hard they was practicing anyway. Every day, Jean and Laura was up at dawn to practice. When the big day finally come, they received a lot of atention when they came in first and second in the competition. Patricia Loomis came in third.

Jean and Laura were determined to enter the diving contest, even though the reigning champion, Patricia Loomis, said they had no possibility of winning against her. It's amazing how hard they were practicing anyway. Every day, Jean and Laura were up at dawn to practice. When the big day finally came, they received a lot of attention when they came in first and second in the competition. Patricia Loomis came in third.

Unit 3 Week 18 Day 1

1. Last year Priscilla wasnt able to ski with her friends.
2. She didnt have enough strength in her knees.
3. Now Priscilla is better, and she doesnt miss a chance to go skiing.

1. Last year, Priscilla wasn't able to ski with her friends.
2. She didn't have enough strength in her knees.
3. Now Priscilla is better, and she doesn't miss a chance to go skiing.

Unit 3 Week 18 Day 2

1. Wally didnt think he could find his way home in the blizzard.
2. He hadnt ever seen it snow this hard.
3. Even though Wally wasnt able to see five feet ahead of him, he knew he must keep going.

1. Wally didn't think he could find his way home in the blizzard.
2. He hadn't ever seen it snow this hard.
3. Even though Wally wasn't able to see five feet ahead of him, he knew he must keep going.

Unit 3 Week 18 Day 3

1. Bob hasnt ever beaten Lori at checkers.
2. He doesnt know how she wins all the time.
3. Bob believes that he will beat Lori sooner or later, so he isnt giving up.

1. Bob hasn't ever beaten Lori at checkers.
2. He doesn't know how she wins all the time.
3. Bob believes that we will beat Lori sooner or later, so he isn't giving up.

Unit 3 Week 18 Day 4

1. Barbara are going to play the violin in the school contest.
2. She ain't going to let her fear stop her.
3. She know she can do it.

1. Barbara is going to play the violin in the school contest.
2. She isn't going to let her fear stop her.
3. She knows she can do it.

Unit 3 Week 18 Day 5

1. Everyone says I ain't going to make the softball team.
2. I is determined to show them I can do it.
3. I is working hard and practicing my swing every day.

1. Everyone says I am not going to make the softball team.
2. I am determined to show them I can do it.
3. I am working hard and practicing my swing every day.

REVIEW PARAGRAPHS FOR PROOFREADING

Ramón wanted to go on a five-state bicycle tour, but he wasnt sure he were strong enough. A bike trip through Virmont, New Hampshure, Mane, Rode Islend, and Masachussetts would be quite a challenge! He hadnt done anything like that before.

Finally Ramón decided to go on the tour. After six days, he started to feel very tired. He didnt think he could continue. "I ain't giving up," he told himself.

Day after day, Ramón kept bicycling. At the end of the tour, he felt good that he had finished the trip. "I feeling proud," Ramón told the tour leader. "I havent felt this good in a long, long time."

Ramón wanted to go on a five-state bicycle tour, but he wasn't sure he was strong enough. A bike trip through Vermont, New Hampshire, Maine, Rhode Island, and Massachusetts would be quite a challenge! He hadn't done anything like that before.

Finally, Ramón decided to go on the tour. After six days, he started to feel very tired. He didn't think he could continue. "I am not giving up," he told himself.

Day after day, Ramón kept bicycling. At the end of the tour, he felt good that he had finished the trip. "I feel proud," Ramón told the tour leader. "I haven't felt this good in a long, long time."

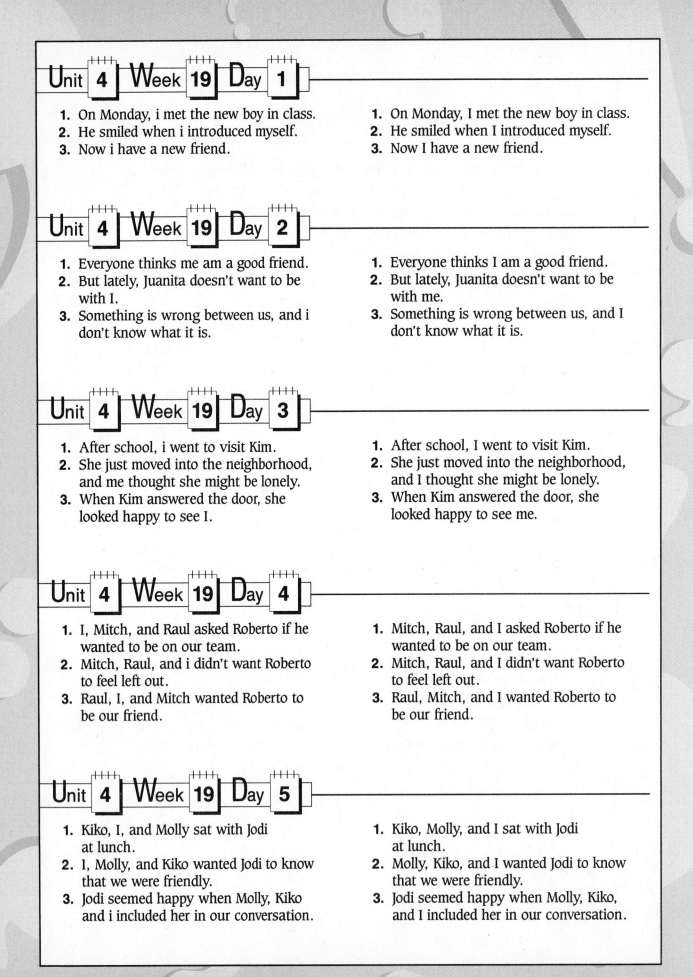

Unit 4 | Week 19 | Day 1

1. On Monday, i met the new boy in class.
2. He smiled when i introduced myself.
3. Now i have a new friend.

1. On Monday, I met the new boy in class.
2. He smiled when I introduced myself.
3. Now I have a new friend.

Unit 4 | Week 19 | Day 2

1. Everyone thinks me am a good friend.
2. But lately, Juanita doesn't want to be with I.
3. Something is wrong between us, and i don't know what it is.

1. Everyone thinks I am a good friend.
2. But lately, Juanita doesn't want to be with me.
3. Something is wrong between us, and I don't know what it is.

Unit 4 | Week 19 | Day 3

1. After school, i went to visit Kim.
2. She just moved into the neighborhood, and me thought she might be lonely.
3. When Kim answered the door, she looked happy to see I.

1. After school, I went to visit Kim.
2. She just moved into the neighborhood, and I thought she might be lonely.
3. When Kim answered the door, she looked happy to see me.

Unit 4 | Week 19 | Day 4

1. I, Mitch, and Raul asked Roberto if he wanted to be on our team.
2. Mitch, Raul, and i didn't want Roberto to feel left out.
3. Raul, I, and Mitch wanted Roberto to be our friend.

1. Mitch, Raul, and I asked Roberto if he wanted to be on our team.
2. Mitch, Raul, and I didn't want Roberto to feel left out.
3. Raul, Mitch, and I wanted Roberto to be our friend.

Unit 4 | Week 19 | Day 5

1. Kiko, I, and Molly sat with Jodi at lunch.
2. I, Molly, and Kiko wanted Jodi to know that we were friendly.
3. Jodi seemed happy when Molly, Kiko and i included her in our conversation.

1. Kiko, Molly, and I sat with Jodi at lunch.
2. Molly, Kiko, and I wanted Jodi to know that we were friendly.
3. Jodi seemed happy when Molly, Kiko, and I included her in our conversation.

REVIEW PARAGRAPHS FOR PROOFREADING

As i picked berries from the razberry bush me noticed a tiny kitten looking up at I. It was crying. I picked up the kitten, wrapped it in my skarf, and brought it into the house. When my little sister saw the kitten she squealed. "Ooh! Give it to I," she said. "I'll feed it some fruit."

"Wait a minute," me said. "First let's discus the things that newborn kittens do and don't eat. They don't eat cantelope, and they don't eat watermellon. They don't eat fruit at all! They drink milk."

As we got ready to feed milk to the kitten, I thought how much fun it would be getting to know this adorable little creature. Me hoped my parents would let I keep it for a pet.

As I picked berries from the raspberry bush, I noticed a tiny kitten looking up at me. It was crying. I picked up the kitten, wrapped it in my scarf, and brought it into the house. When my little sister saw the kitten she squealed. "Ooh! Give it to me," she said. "I'll feed it some fruit."

"Wait a minute," I said. "First, let's discuss the things that newborn kittens do and don't eat. They don't eat cantaloupe, and they don't eat watermelon. They don't eat fruit at all! They drink milk."

As we got ready to feed milk to the kitten, I thought how much fun it would be getting to know this adorable little creature. I hoped my parents would let me keep it for a pet.

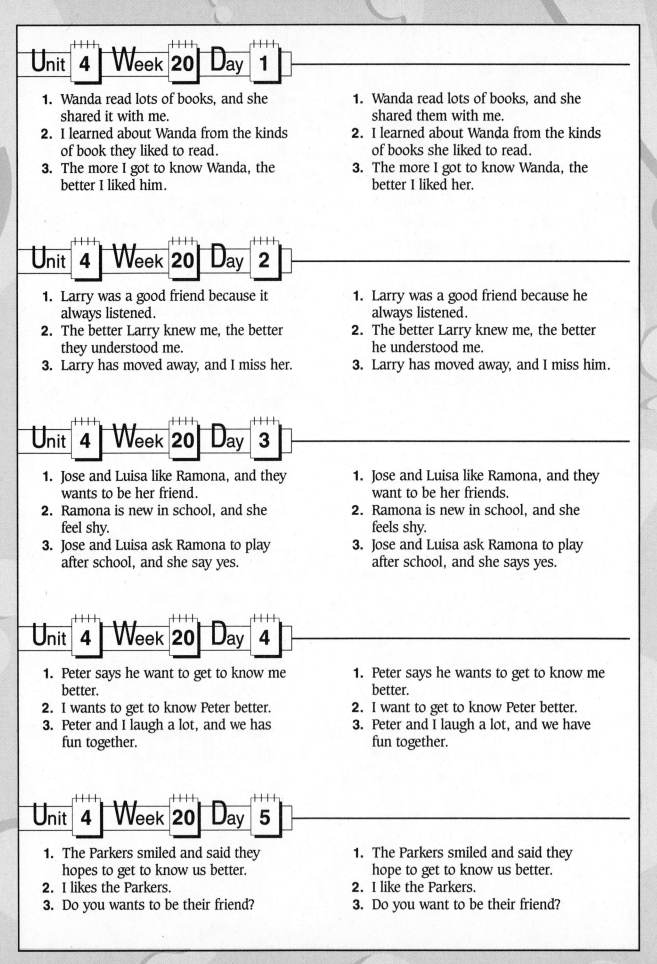

Unit 4 | Week 20 | Day 1

1. Wanda read lots of books, and she shared it with me.
2. I learned about Wanda from the kinds of book they liked to read.
3. The more I got to know Wanda, the better I liked him.

1. Wanda read lots of books, and she shared them with me.
2. I learned about Wanda from the kinds of books she liked to read.
3. The more I got to know Wanda, the better I liked her.

Unit 4 | Week 20 | Day 2

1. Larry was a good friend because it always listened.
2. The better Larry knew me, the better they understood me.
3. Larry has moved away, and I miss her.

1. Larry was a good friend because he always listened.
2. The better Larry knew me, the better he understood me.
3. Larry has moved away, and I miss him.

Unit 4 | Week 20 | Day 3

1. Jose and Luisa like Ramona, and they wants to be her friend.
2. Ramona is new in school, and she feel shy.
3. Jose and Luisa ask Ramona to play after school, and she say yes.

1. Jose and Luisa like Ramona, and they want to be her friends.
2. Ramona is new in school, and she feels shy.
3. Jose and Luisa ask Ramona to play after school, and she says yes.

Unit 4 | Week 20 | Day 4

1. Peter says he want to get to know me better.
2. I wants to get to know Peter better.
3. Peter and I laugh a lot, and we has fun together.

1. Peter says he wants to get to know me better.
2. I want to get to know Peter better.
3. Peter and I laugh a lot, and we have fun together.

Unit 4 | Week 20 | Day 5

1. The Parkers smiled and said they hopes to get to know us better.
2. I likes the Parkers.
3. Do you wants to be their friend?

1. The Parkers smiled and said they hope to get to know us better.
2. I like the Parkers.
3. Do you want to be their friend?

REVIEW PARAGRAPH FOR PROOFREADING

Mary Johnson put the bundle of paper down on their desk. "This mystery novle is teriffic!" she said to the editer who was his boss. "It have an exciting plot. It are fast-paced and suspenseful. I was terified as I was reading it. The author did an especially good job describing the appearence, thoughts, and actions of the main character. As a result, I feel I really knows Detective Walsh well. I loves the book, and I am sure that fifth- and sixth-graders will love them too!"

Mary Johnson put the bundle of paper down on her desk. "This mystery novel is terrific!" she said to the editor who was her boss. "It has an exciting plot. It is fast-paced and suspenseful. I was terrified as I was reading it. The author did an especially good job describing the appearance, thoughts, and actions of the main character. As a result, I feel I really know Detective Walsh well. I love the book, and I am sure that fifth- and sixth-graders will love it, too!"

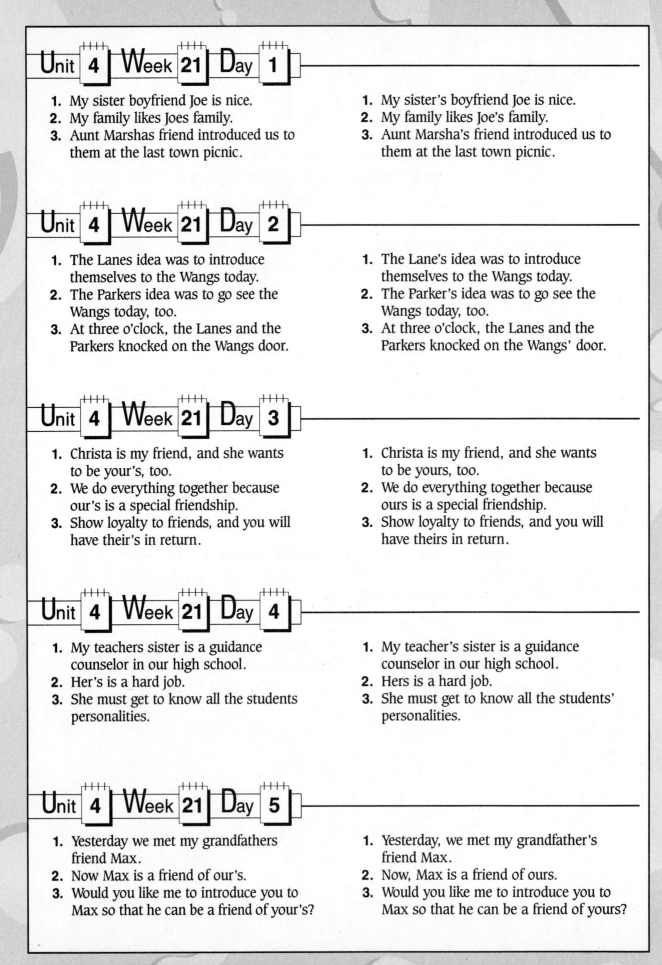

Unit 4 | Week 21 | Day 1

1. My sister boyfriend Joe is nice.
2. My family likes Joes family.
3. Aunt Marshas friend introduced us to them at the last town picnic.

1. My sister's boyfriend Joe is nice.
2. My family likes Joe's family.
3. Aunt Marsha's friend introduced us to them at the last town picnic.

Unit 4 | Week 21 | Day 2

1. The Lanes idea was to introduce themselves to the Wangs today.
2. The Parkers idea was to go see the Wangs today, too.
3. At three o'clock, the Lanes and the Parkers knocked on the Wangs door.

1. The Lane's idea was to introduce themselves to the Wangs today.
2. The Parker's idea was to go see the Wangs today, too.
3. At three o'clock, the Lanes and the Parkers knocked on the Wangs' door.

Unit 4 | Week 21 | Day 3

1. Christa is my friend, and she wants to be your's, too.
2. We do everything together because our's is a special friendship.
3. Show loyalty to friends, and you will have their's in return.

1. Christa is my friend, and she wants to be yours, too.
2. We do everything together because ours is a special friendship.
3. Show loyalty to friends, and you will have theirs in return.

Unit 4 | Week 21 | Day 4

1. My teachers sister is a guidance counselor in our high school.
2. Her's is a hard job.
3. She must get to know all the students personalities.

1. My teacher's sister is a guidance counselor in our high school.
2. Hers is a hard job.
3. She must get to know all the students' personalities.

Unit 4 | Week 21 | Day 5

1. Yesterday we met my grandfathers friend Max.
2. Now Max is a friend of our's.
3. Would you like me to introduce you to Max so that he can be a friend of your's?

1. Yesterday, we met my grandfather's friend Max.
2. Now, Max is a friend of ours.
3. Would you like me to introduce you to Max so that he can be a friend of yours?

REVIEW PARAGRAPHS FOR PROOFREADING

Martin walked into the splended chirch. The candles flames flickered brightly, and he saw a begger in one corner. The womans shoulders were hunched, and her coller was dirty. Her head was bair, and one glove lay in the aisle.

"You dropped your glove," Martin said. "It's on the floor."

"Thank you," the woman said, looking up at Martin. "Your's is the kindest face I have ever seen." A tear came to the womans eyes, and Martin decided to get to know her.

He learned that the woman had no family or friends. Her's was a hard and tragic life. As he listened, Martin knew that he would never forget this woman.

Martin walked into the splendid church. The candles' flames flickered brightly, and he saw a beggar in one corner. The woman's shoulders were hunched, and her collar was dirty. Her head was bare, and one glove lay in the aisle.

"You dropped your glove," Martin said. "It's on the floor."

"Thank you," the woman said, looking up at Martin. "Yours is the kindest face I have ever seen." A tear came to the woman's eyes, and Martin decided to get to know her.

He learned that the woman had no family or friends. Hers was a hard and tragic life. As he listened, Martin knew that he would never forget this woman.

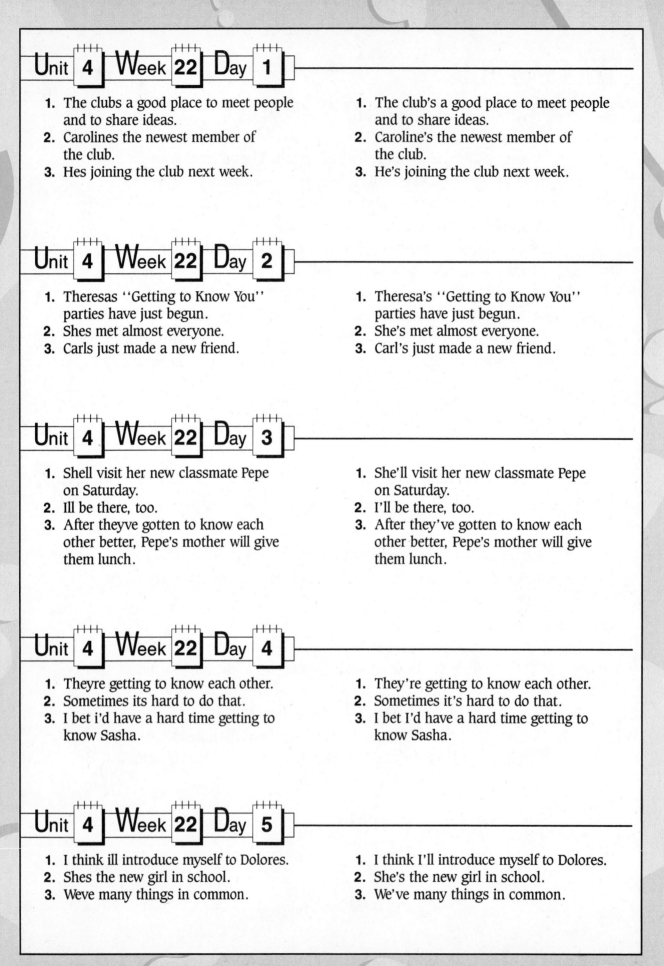

Unit 4 | Week 22 | Day 1

1. The clubs a good place to meet people and to share ideas.
2. Carolines the newest member of the club.
3. Hes joining the club next week.

1. The club's a good place to meet people and to share ideas.
2. Caroline's the newest member of the club.
3. He's joining the club next week.

Unit 4 | Week 22 | Day 2

1. Theresas "Getting to Know You" parties have just begun.
2. Shes met almost everyone.
3. Carls just made a new friend.

1. Theresa's "Getting to Know You" parties have just begun.
2. She's met almost everyone.
3. Carl's just made a new friend.

Unit 4 | Week 22 | Day 3

1. Shell visit her new classmate Pepe on Saturday.
2. Ill be there, too.
3. After theyve gotten to know each other better, Pepe's mother will give them lunch.

1. She'll visit her new classmate Pepe on Saturday.
2. I'll be there, too.
3. After they've gotten to know each other better, Pepe's mother will give them lunch.

Unit 4 | Week 22 | Day 4

1. Theyre getting to know each other.
2. Sometimes its hard to do that.
3. I bet i'd have a hard time getting to know Sasha.

1. They're getting to know each other.
2. Sometimes it's hard to do that.
3. I bet I'd have a hard time getting to know Sasha.

Unit 4 | Week 22 | Day 5

1. I think ill introduce myself to Dolores.
2. Shes the new girl in school.
3. Weve many things in common.

1. I think I'll introduce myself to Dolores.
2. She's the new girl in school.
3. We've many things in common.

REVIEW PARAGRAPH FOR PROOFREADING

I traveled to the Carribean recently. Ive never been they're before, but its always been my Aunt Stella's favorate place. Shes always raved about the beautiful sonsets there. I went during festivel time. Youd have loved it. We had a wonderful banket almost every night.

I traveled to the Caribbean recently. I've never been there before, but it's always been my Aunt Stella's favorite place. She's always raved about the beautiful sunsets there. I went during festival time. You'd have loved it. We had a wonderful banquet almost every night.

Unit 4 | Week 23 | Day 1

1. On Wednesday, i met Patrick during recess.
2. When i asked him where he was from, he said he had just moved from Texas.
3. Patrick and i are now good friends.

1. On Wednesday, I met Patrick during recess.
2. When I asked him where he was from, he said he had just moved from Texas.
3. Patrick and I are now good friends.

Unit 4 | Week 23 | Day 2

1. My parents think i should get to know Sachiko better.
2. I wonder if Sachiko wants to get to know I.
3. Maybe Sachiko and me could become friends.

1. My parents think I should get to know Sachiko better.
2. I wonder if Sachiko wants to get to know me.
3. Maybe Sachiko and I could become friends.

Unit 4 | Week 23 | Day 3

1. Kevin and me enjoy doing things together.
2. Now Mario wants to do things with Kevin and I.
3. Kevin and i would like to get to know Mario better, so we invited him to go fishing.

1. Kevin and I enjoy doing things together.
2. Now Mario wants to do things with Kevin and me.
3. Kevin and I would like to get to know Mario better, so we invited him to go fishing.

Unit 4 | Week 23 | Day 4

1. I like being with Martha, and it likes being with me.
2. At first, Martha was shy, but now he is friendly.
3. Martha likes to play tag and hopscotch, and we play it often.

1. I like being with Martha, and she likes being with me.
2. At first, Martha was shy, but now she is friendly.
3. Martha likes to play tag and hopscotch, and we play them often.

Unit 4 | Week 23 | Day 5

1. Juan says he want us to get to know each other better.
2. I tells him we should eat lunch together in the cafeteria.
3. During lunch, Juan and I found out that we has lots in common.

1. Juan says he wants us to get to know each other better.
2. I tell him we should eat lunch together in the cafeteria.
3. During lunch, Juan and I found out that we have lots in common.

REVIEW PARAGRAPHS FOR PROOFREADING

My edditor, Karen Jones, called I into her office. He wanted to disscus their novil about two people who meet on a Caribbeun vacation. ''Your story is splended,'' she said. ''However, you must tell more about how the main characters get to know each other.''

At first, I were puzzled because i thought me had done a good job with the main characters. However, when Karen explained to i what they wanted me to do, I knew she was right.

I followed Karen's suggestions, and my book became a bestseller.

My editor, Karen Jones, called me into her office. She wanted to discuss my novel about two people who meet on a Caribbean vacation. ''Your story is splendid,'' she said. ''However, you must tell more about how the main characters get to know each other.''

At first, I was puzzled because I thought I had done a good job with the main characters. However, when Karen explained to me what she wanted me to do, I knew she was right.

I followed Karen's suggestions, and my book became a bestseller.

Unit 4 Week 24 Day 1

1. My brothers girlfriend Nancy Pace is friendly.
2. The Paces house is down the street.
3. I would like to get to know Nancys brother Carl.

1. My brother's girlfriend, Nancy Pace, is friendly.
2. The Paces' house is down the street.
3. I would like to get to know Nancy's brother Carl.

Unit 4 Week 24 Day 2

1. My aunts cousins Leroy and Jackson are gym teachers at our junior high school.
2. Their's is a challenging job.
3. They must get to know the students strengths and weaknesses and be sure that the students don't get hurt.

1. My aunt's cousins Leroy and Jackson are gym teachers at our junior high school.
2. Theirs is a challenging job.
3. They must get to know the students' strengths and weaknesses and be sure that the students don't get hurt.

Unit 4 Week 24 Day 3

1. Last week we met the storeowners son Ted.
2. Ted has become a friend of our's.
3. After we introduced Ted to Mike and Ralph, Ted said he wanted to become a friend of their's, too.

1. Last week, we met the storeowners' son Ted.
2. Ted has become a friend of ours.
3. After we introduced Ted to Mike and Ralph, Ted said he wanted to become a friend of theirs, too.

Unit 4 Week 24 Day 4

1. Shell make more friends when school starts in the fall.
2. Hes made friends on his block already.
3. Jims the kind of person others want to get to know.

1. She'll make more friends when school starts in the fall.
2. He's made friends on his block already.
3. Jim's the kind of person others want to get to know.

Unit 4 Week 24 Day 5

1. Im not ready to meet my baby sister.
2. Shes so small.
3. I hope well be friends someday.

1. I'm not ready to meet my baby sister.
2. She's so small.
3. I hope we'll be friends someday.

Review Paragraph for Proofreading

Today, Maureen is joining a club for students who have just moved to the neighborhood from different states. Its the kind of club in which the members can talk about their old hometowns and make plans to explore they're new town. In the club are students from Arkansis, Indeana, Mishigan, Ilinois, and Iowah. Their planning to have a group picnic so that all the members can tell about themselves. Maureen believes shell be happy in the club.

Today, Maureen is joining a club for students who have just moved to the neighborhood from different states. It's the kind of club in which the members can talk about their old hometowns and make plans to explore their new town. In the club are students from Arkansas, Indiana, Michigan, Illinois, and Iowa. They're planning to have a group picnic so that all the members can tell about themselves. Maureen believes she'll be happy in the club.

Unit 5 | Week 25 | Day 1

1. The buildings I saw in New York City were biggest than the ones I saw in Charleston.
2. The buildings in New York looked like the taller buildings in the world.
3. However, my mother said that the taller building in the world is in Chicago.

1. The buildings I saw in New York City were bigger than the ones I saw in Charleston.
2. The buildings in New York looked like the tallest buildings in the world.
3. However, my mother said that the tallest building in the world is in Chicago.

Unit 5 | Week 25 | Day 2

1. Cleo thinks that the beaches in California are best than the beaches in Florida.
2. She had most fun at the beaches in California than she did at the ones in Florida.
3. Cleo thinks that the beaches in California are the better beaches in the United States.

1. Cleo thinks that the beaches in California are better than the beaches in Florida.
2. She had more fun at the beaches in California than she did at the ones in Florida.
3. Cleo thinks that the beaches in California are the best beaches in the United States.

Unit 5 | Week 25 | Day 3

1. The sightseeing bus I was in moved slowest than the train on the tracks nearby.
2. The train moved slowest than the plane that zoomed above us.
3. The plane moved the faster of all.

1. The sightseeing bus I was in moved slower than the train on the tracks nearby.
2. The train moved slower than the plane that zoomed above us.
3. The plane moved the fastest of all.

Unit 5 | Week 25 | Day 4

1. During my visit to Texas, I discovered that I sleep best on a plane than I do on a train.
2. I sleep worst on the train than on the plane because the train ride is bumpier.
3. Of all the places to sleep, I sleep better in my bed.

1. During my visit to Texas, I discovered that I sleep better on a plane than I do on a train.
2. I sleep worse on the train than on the plane because the train ride is bumpier.
3. Of all the places to sleep, I sleep best in my bed.

Unit 5 | Week 25 | Day 5

1. Pam thinks that mountains are prettiest than seashores.
2. Ted thinks that seashores are the prettier vacation places a person can visit.
3. On our last visit to the shore, Pam swam faster than I did, but Ted swam the faster of us all.

1. Pam thinks that mountains are prettier than seashores.
2. Ted thinks that seashores are the prettiest vacation places a person can visit.
3. On our last visit to the shore, Pam swam faster that I did, but Ted swam the fastest of us all.

REVIEW PARAGRAPH FOR PROOFREADING

The motorcicle was the most biggest I had ever seen. There was simply no compareson with the dozin others in the race. When the race began, the aplause was the more thunderous I had ever heard. When the rider of the huger bike passed the quater-mile mark, she was in the lead. We knew she would win.

The motorcycle was the biggest I had ever seen. There was simply no comparison with the dozen others in the race. When the race began, the applause was the most thunderous I had ever heard. When the rider of the huge bike passed the quarter-mile mark, she was in the lead. We knew she would win.

Unit 5 | Week 26 | Day 1

1. Last week, I took an trip to Yellowstone National Park.
2. A interesting fact I learned is that Yellowstone is the oldest national park in the United States.
3. In 1988, an series of fires caused much of Yellowstone to burn.

1. Last week, I took a trip to Yellowstone National Park.
2. An interesting fact I learned is that Yellowstone is the oldest national park in the United States.
3. In 1988, a series of fires caused much of Yellowstone to burn.

Unit 5 | Week 26 | Day 2

1. In Alaska, we saw Mt. McKinley, a tallest mountain in North America.
2. We learned that Alaska was once an possession of Russia.
3. A adventure in Alaska is a must for everyone.

1. In Alaska, we saw Mt. McKinley, the tallest mountain in North America.
2. We learned that Alaska was once a possession of Russia.
3. An adventure in Alaska is a must for everyone.

Unit 5 | Week 26 | Day 3

1. I like to ride in a airplane.
2. I took an plane to get to Massachusetts.
3. It was a most exciting trip I ever took!

1. I like to ride in an airplane.
2. I took a plane to get to Massachusetts.
3. It was the most exciting trip I ever took!

Unit 5 | Week 26 | Day 4

1. Our european vacation was filled with new and exciting experiences.
2. Our first stop was England, where we explored the english countryside.
3. Then we visited scottish castles before traveling to France.

1. Our European vacation was filled with new and exciting experiences.
2. Our first stop was England, where we explored the English countryside.
3. Then we visited Scottish castles before traveling to France.

Unit 5 | Week 26 | Day 5

1. While traveling through the Far East, I discovered the japanese art of flower arranging.
2. I also saw many fine examples of chinese porcelain.
3. The thing I enjoyed most of all was the fashion show of traditional korean costumes.

1. While traveling through the Far East, I discovered the Japanese art of flower arranging.
2. I also saw many fine examples of Chinese porcelain.
3. The thing I enjoyed most of all was the fashion show of traditional Korean costumes.

REVIEW PARAGRAPHS FOR PROOFREADING

An day for my white-water raft trip had come. I and ten swiss tourists would travel on one raft down a Colorado River. Even though we all could understand and speak English, I heard conversations in different languages. I heard german words, french exclamations, and italian phrases. I never knew the Swiss spoke so many languages!

Just before we left, our skilful trip leader gave an little speech. She told us to be carefull climbing into our raft. She warned us to be alirt and causious throughout our journey. Listening to her, I became more and more excited. My chest pounded, and I had an funny qiver in my stomach. This was going to be quite a adventure!

The day for my white-water raft trip had come. I and ten Swiss tourists would travel on one raft down the Colorado River. Even though we all could understand and speak English, I heard conversations in different languages. I heard German words, French exclamations, and Italian phrases. I never knew the Swiss spoke so many languages!

Just before we left, our skillful trip leader gave a little speech. She told us to be careful climbing into our raft. She warned us to be alert and cautious throughout our journey. Listening to her, I became more and more excited. My chest pounded, and I had a funny quiver in my stomach. This was going to be quite an adventure!

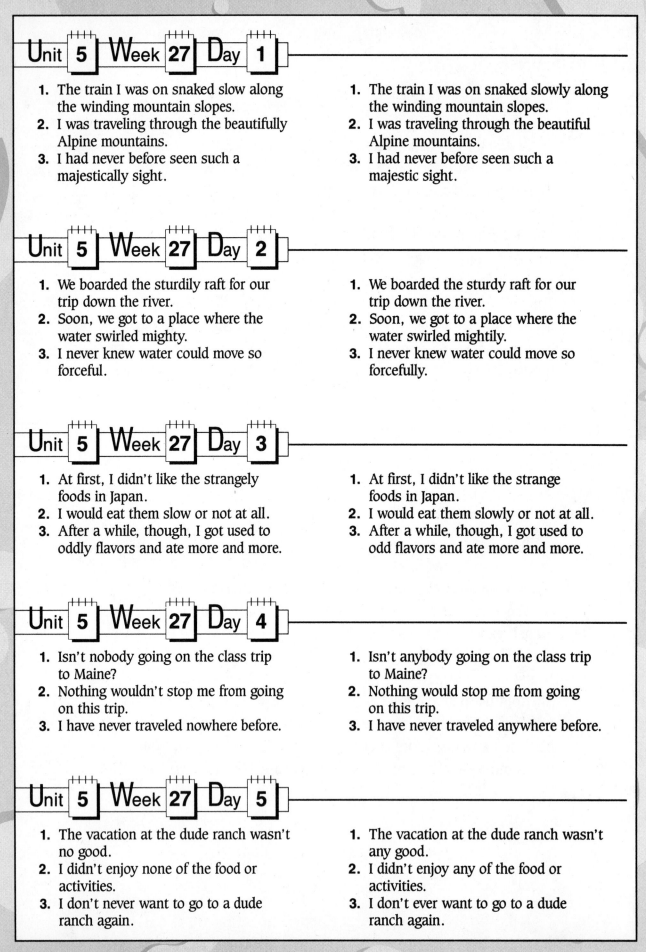

Unit 5 Week 27 Day 1

1. The train I was on snaked slow along the winding mountain slopes.
2. I was traveling through the beautifully Alpine mountains.
3. I had never before seen such a majestically sight.

1. The train I was on snaked slowly along the winding mountain slopes.
2. I was traveling through the beautiful Alpine mountains.
3. I had never before seen such a majestic sight.

Unit 5 Week 27 Day 2

1. We boarded the sturdily raft for our trip down the river.
2. Soon, we got to a place where the water swirled mighty.
3. I never knew water could move so forceful.

1. We boarded the sturdy raft for our trip down the river.
2. Soon, we got to a place where the water swirled mightily.
3. I never knew water could move so forcefully.

Unit 5 Week 27 Day 3

1. At first, I didn't like the strangely foods in Japan.
2. I would eat them slow or not at all.
3. After a while, though, I got used to oddly flavors and ate more and more.

1. At first, I didn't like the strange foods in Japan.
2. I would eat them slowly or not at all.
3. After a while, though, I got used to odd flavors and ate more and more.

Unit 5 Week 27 Day 4

1. Isn't nobody going on the class trip to Maine?
2. Nothing wouldn't stop me from going on this trip.
3. I have never traveled nowhere before.

1. Isn't anybody going on the class trip to Maine?
2. Nothing would stop me from going on this trip.
3. I have never traveled anywhere before.

Unit 5 Week 27 Day 5

1. The vacation at the dude ranch wasn't no good.
2. I didn't enjoy none of the food or activities.
3. I don't never want to go to a dude ranch again.

1. The vacation at the dude ranch wasn't any good.
2. I didn't enjoy any of the food or activities.
3. I don't ever want to go to a dude ranch again.

REVIEW PARAGRAPH FOR PROOFREADING

While visiting Gettysburg, Pennsylvania, I saw a movie of one of the most famous battles of the Civil War. Two characters from the movie stand out sharp in my mind. One was a sergeant who carried a rifel, and the other was a captain who carried a pistel. You could see the pain in the sadly eyes of both men as they looked at each other across the battlefield. You could see their hands trembel violent as they aimed their weapons at each other. Then the sound of gunfire filled the air. There was a loudly grone and then a softly mone. The captain fell to the ground.

While visiting Gettysburg, Pennsylvania, I saw a movie of one of the most famous battles of the Civil War. Two characters from the movie stand out sharply in my mind. One was a sergeant who carried a rifle, and the other was a captain who carried a pistol. You could see the pain in the sad eyes of both men as they looked at each other across the battlefield. You could see their hands tremble violently as they aimed their weapons at each other. Then the sound of gunfire filled the air. There was a loud groan and then a soft moan. The captain fell to the ground.

Unit 5 Week 28 Day 1

1. Leroy thought that all the beaches in Hawaii were large smooth and crowded.
2. When he got there, he was surprised to learn that many of the beaches are small rocky and empty.
3. It was true, though, that the water was blue clean and warm.

1. Leroy thought that all the beaches in Hawaii were large, smooth, and crowded.
2. When he got there, he was surprised to learn that many of the beaches are small, rocky, and empty.
3. It was true, though, that the water was blue, clean, and warm.

Unit 5 Week 28 Day 2

1. Justin discovered that many streets in New York City are noisy narrow and crowded.
2. He learned that the people who live in the city are kind friendly and helpful.
3. Justin decided that New York City is an exciting interesting and fun place to visit.

1. Justin discovered that many streets in New York City are noisy, narrow, and crowded.
2. He learned that the people who live in the city are kind, friendly, and helpful.
3. Justin decided that New York City is an exciting, interesting, and fun place to visit.

Unit 5 Week 28 Day 3

1. On their vacation in Hawaii, Lou's family saw waterfalls mountains and volcanoes.
2. They visited museums beaches and parks.
3. They ate lots of pineapple papayas and bananas.

1. On their vacation in Hawaii, Lou's family saw waterfalls, mountains, and volcanoes.
2. They visited museums, beaches, and parks.
3. They ate lots of pineapple, papayas, and bananas.

Unit 5 Week 28 Day 4

1. During his trip to Switzerland, Renaldo rode in a cable car sailed in a boat and walked along a lake.
2. He enjoyed singing dancing and playing the alphorn.
3. Renaldo's brother frowned cried and stamped his feet when it came time to go home.

1. During his trip to Switzerland, Renaldo rode in a cable car, sailed in a boat, and walked along a lake.
2. He enjoyed singing, dancing, and playing the alphorn.
3. Renaldo's brother frowned, cried, and stamped his feet when it came time to go home.

Unit 5 Week 28 Day 5

1. We traveled in Holland France and Belgium.
2. We rode on boats planes and trains
3. Paris Brussels and Amsterdam are beautiful cities

1. We traveled in Holland, France, and Belgium.
2. We rode on boats, planes, and trains.
3. Paris, Brussels, and Amsterdam are beautiful cities.

REVIEW PARAGRAPH FOR PROOFREADING

Christopher's journey up the Nile River was a hot exhausting and difficult experience. He did not think he could indure the heat servive the food or struggle against the flies much longer. But Christopher was determined not to surender. "This will be over soon," he thought. "Soon I will be home where it is cool. I will be anxous to eat tasty fruits salads and breads again. I just have to hold on for three more days," he thought franticaly.

Christopher's journey up the Nile River was a hot, exhausting, and difficult experience. He did not think he could endure the heat, survive the food, or struggle against the flies much longer. But Christopher was determined not to surrender. "This will be over soon," he thought. "Soon I will be home where it is cool. I will be anxious to eat tasty fruits, salads, and breads again. I just have to hold on for three more days," he thought frantically.

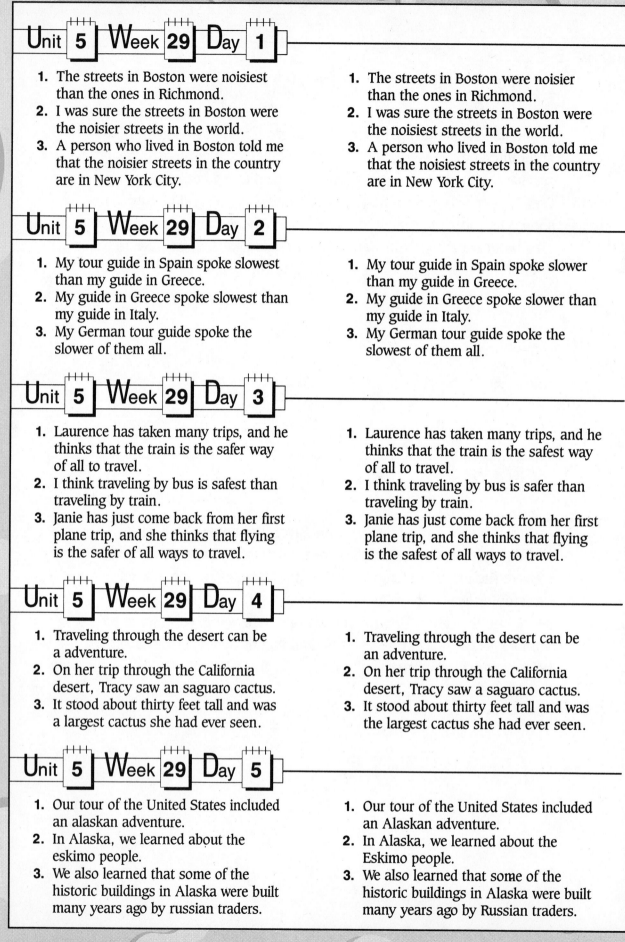

Unit 5 | Week 29 | Day 1

1. The streets in Boston were noisiest than the ones in Richmond.
2. I was sure the streets in Boston were the noisier streets in the world.
3. A person who lived in Boston told me that the noisier streets in the country are in New York City.

1. The streets in Boston were noisier than the ones in Richmond.
2. I was sure the streets in Boston were the noisiest streets in the world.
3. A person who lived in Boston told me that the noisiest streets in the country are in New York City.

Unit 5 | Week 29 | Day 2

1. My tour guide in Spain spoke slowest than my guide in Greece.
2. My guide in Greece spoke slowest than my guide in Italy.
3. My German tour guide spoke the slower of them all.

1. My tour guide in Spain spoke slower than my guide in Greece.
2. My guide in Greece spoke slower than my guide in Italy.
3. My German tour guide spoke the slowest of them all.

Unit 5 | Week 29 | Day 3

1. Laurence has taken many trips, and he thinks that the train is the safer way of all to travel.
2. I think traveling by bus is safest than traveling by train.
3. Janie has just come back from her first plane trip, and she thinks that flying is the safer of all ways to travel.

1. Laurence has taken many trips, and he thinks that the train is the safest way of all to travel.
2. I think traveling by bus is safer than traveling by train.
3. Janie has just come back from her first plane trip, and she thinks that flying is the safest of all ways to travel.

Unit 5 | Week 29 | Day 4

1. Traveling through the desert can be a adventure.
2. On her trip through the California desert, Tracy saw an saguaro cactus.
3. It stood about thirty feet tall and was a largest cactus she had ever seen.

1. Traveling through the desert can be an adventure.
2. On her trip through the California desert, Tracy saw a saguaro cactus.
3. It stood about thirty feet tall and was the largest cactus she had ever seen.

Unit 5 | Week 29 | Day 5

1. Our tour of the United States included an alaskan adventure.
2. In Alaska, we learned about the eskimo people.
3. We also learned that some of the historic buildings in Alaska were built many years ago by russian traders.

1. Our tour of the United States included an Alaskan adventure.
2. In Alaska, we learned about the Eskimo people.
3. We also learned that some of the historic buildings in Alaska were built many years ago by Russian traders.

REVIEW PARAGRAPHS FOR PROOFREADING

Lisa trudged through the snow toward the canadian border. It was the slower she had ever walked in her life. She wasn't sure she could endyure the cold and hunger any longer. Her hands began to trimble. Would she and her family servive the journey to their new home? This trip was even worst than the one they made two years ago. Now her stomach ached from lack of food. Each breath of air caused her chest to hurt.

Suddenly, Lisa heard footsteps behind her. Her hand touched the pistil her father had given her for protection. Her whole body began to qiver. Lisa turned around to face the bigger moose she had ever seen. Lisa froze, and the moose darted away. It moved quickest than lightning. Lisa had learned what it meant to face danger.

Lisa trudged through the snow toward the Canadian border. It was the slowest she had ever walked in her life. She wasn't sure she could endure the cold and hunger any longer. Her hands began to tremble. Would she and her family survive the journey to their new home? This trip was even worse than the one they made two years ago. Now her stomach ached from lack of food. Each breath of air caused her chest to hurt.

Suddenly, Lisa heard footsteps behind her. Her hand touched the pistol her father had given her for protection. Her whole body began to quiver. Lisa turned around to face the biggest moose she had ever seen. Lisa froze, and the moose darted away. It moved quicker than lightning. Lisa had learned what it meant to face danger.

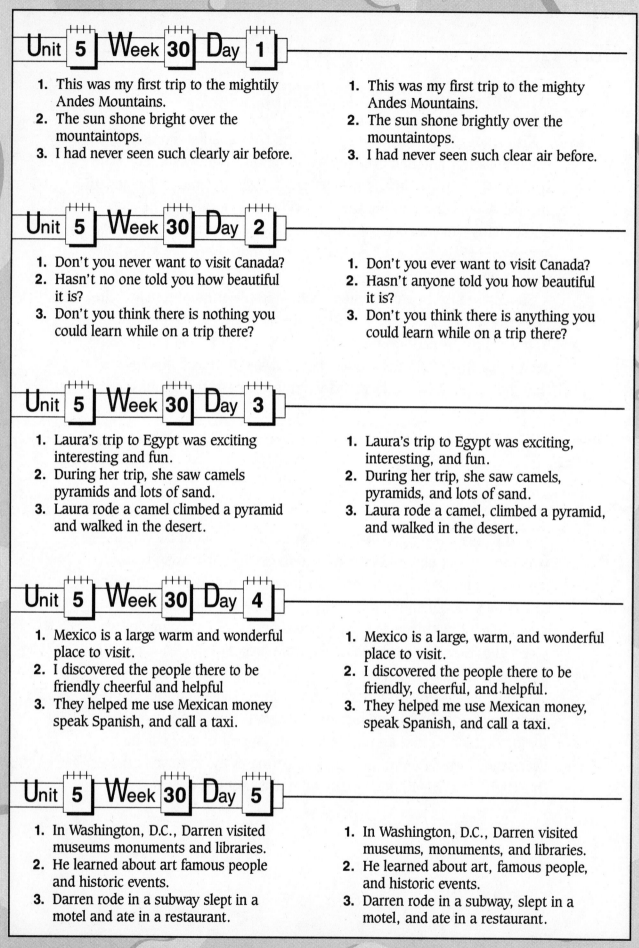

Unit 5 | Week 30 | Day 1

1. This was my first trip to the mightily Andes Mountains.
2. The sun shone bright over the mountaintops.
3. I had never seen such clearly air before.

1. This was my first trip to the mighty Andes Mountains.
2. The sun shone brightly over the mountaintops.
3. I had never seen such clear air before.

Unit 5 | Week 30 | Day 2

1. Don't you never want to visit Canada?
2. Hasn't no one told you how beautiful it is?
3. Don't you think there is nothing you could learn while on a trip there?

1. Don't you ever want to visit Canada?
2. Hasn't anyone told you how beautiful it is?
3. Don't you think there is anything you could learn while on a trip there?

Unit 5 | Week 30 | Day 3

1. Laura's trip to Egypt was exciting interesting and fun.
2. During her trip, she saw camels pyramids and lots of sand.
3. Laura rode a camel climbed a pyramid and walked in the desert.

1. Laura's trip to Egypt was exciting, interesting, and fun.
2. During her trip, she saw camels, pyramids, and lots of sand.
3. Laura rode a camel, climbed a pyramid, and walked in the desert.

Unit 5 | Week 30 | Day 4

1. Mexico is a large warm and wonderful place to visit.
2. I discovered the people there to be friendly cheerful and helpful
3. They helped me use Mexican money speak Spanish, and call a taxi.

1. Mexico is a large, warm, and wonderful place to visit.
2. I discovered the people there to be friendly, cheerful, and helpful.
3. They helped me use Mexican money, speak Spanish, and call a taxi.

Unit 5 | Week 30 | Day 5

1. In Washington, D.C., Darren visited museums monuments and libraries.
2. He learned about art famous people and historic events.
3. Darren rode in a subway slept in a motel and ate in a restaurant.

1. In Washington, D.C., Darren visited museums, monuments, and libraries.
2. He learned about art, famous people, and historic events.
3. Darren rode in a subway, slept in a motel, and ate in a restaurant.

REVIEW PARAGRAPH FOR PROOFREADING

During my recently trip to Washington, D.C., I visited the Senate. There I met the representatives of the states of Jeorgia, Alebama, and Floreda. I shook hands with the busily senators, and we talked happy for just a few minutes. They told me how they help make laws meet leaders from other countries and assist the people from their home states. I learned a lot from talking with the senators. When I get older, I want to be a senator, too. Perhaps I will represent Kansis or Nebrasca.

During my recent trip to Washington, D.C., I visited the Senate. There I met the representatives of the states of Georgia, Alabama, and Florida. I shook hands with the busy senators, and we talked happily for just a few minutes. They told me how they help make laws, meet leaders from other countries, and assist the people from their home states. I learned a lot from talking with the senators. When I get older, I want to be a senator, too. Perhaps I will represent Kansas or Nebraska.

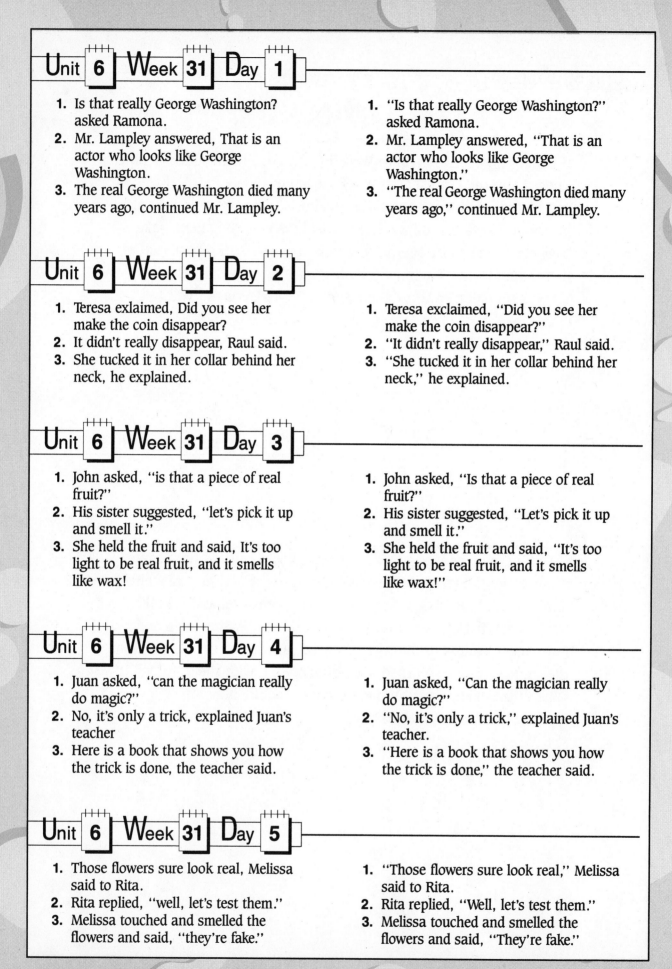

Unit 6 Week 31 Day 1

1. Is that really George Washington? asked Ramona.
2. Mr. Lampley answered, That is an actor who looks like George Washington.
3. The real George Washington died many years ago, continued Mr. Lampley.

1. "Is that really George Washington?" asked Ramona.
2. Mr. Lampley answered, "That is an actor who looks like George Washington."
3. "The real George Washington died many years ago," continued Mr. Lampley.

Unit 6 Week 31 Day 2

1. Teresa exlaimed, Did you see her make the coin disappear?
2. It didn't really disappear, Raul said.
3. She tucked it in her collar behind her neck, he explained.

1. Teresa exclaimed, "Did you see her make the coin disappear?"
2. "It didn't really disappear," Raul said.
3. "She tucked it in her collar behind her neck," he explained.

Unit 6 Week 31 Day 3

1. John asked, "is that a piece of real fruit?"
2. His sister suggested, "let's pick it up and smell it."
3. She held the fruit and said, It's too light to be real fruit, and it smells like wax!

1. John asked, "Is that a piece of real fruit?"
2. His sister suggested, "Let's pick it up and smell it."
3. She held the fruit and said, "It's too light to be real fruit, and it smells like wax!"

Unit 6 Week 31 Day 4

1. Juan asked, "can the magician really do magic?"
2. No, it's only a trick, explained Juan's teacher
3. Here is a book that shows you how the trick is done, the teacher said.

1. Juan asked, "Can the magician really do magic?"
2. "No, it's only a trick," explained Juan's teacher.
3. "Here is a book that shows you how the trick is done," the teacher said.

Unit 6 Week 31 Day 5

1. Those flowers sure look real, Melissa said to Rita.
2. Rita replied, "well, let's test them."
3. Melissa touched and smelled the flowers and said, "they're fake."

1. "Those flowers sure look real," Melissa said to Rita.
2. Rita replied, "Well, let's test them."
3. Melissa touched and smelled the flowers and said, "They're fake."

REVIEW PARAGRAPHS FOR PROOFREADING

Mrs. Joslin said, "today we are going to do an experament to prove that white light is made up of different colors."

Wait a minute. That can't be, said Willie.

Hold this prism up against the light and look through it, Willie, Mrs. Joslin said. "Tell me what you observe."

"I see colors!" exclaimed the amazed boy.

"That's right," Mrs. Joslin said. "now each of you look through the prism. Then use crayons and white paper to record what you see. Your assinment is to mark the colors in the order they appear."

Why is that important? Thelma asked.

Mrs. Joslin explained, "a good sceintist always makes sure to take notes that are acurrate. Now get to it!"

The class began to investegate in earnest.

Mrs. Joslin said, "Today we are going to do an experiment to prove that white light is made up of different colors."

"Wait a minute. That can't be," said Willie.

"Hold this prism up against the light and look through it, Willie," Mrs. Joslin said. "Tell me what you observe."

"I see colors!" exclaimed the amazed boy.

"That's right," Mrs. Joslin said. "Now each of you look through the prism. Then use crayons and white paper to record what you see. Your assignment is to mark the colors in the order they appear."

"Why is that important?" Thelma asked.

Mrs. Joslin explained, "A good scientist always makes sure to take notes that are accurate. Now, get to it!"

The class began to investigate in earnest.

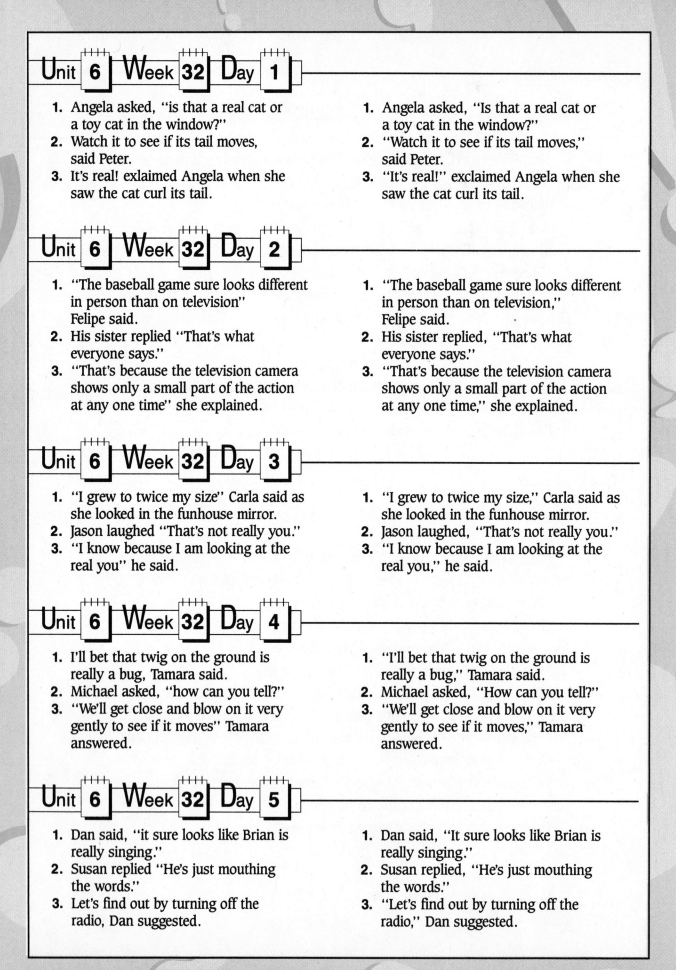

Unit 6 | Week 32 | Day 1

1. Angela asked, "is that a real cat or a toy cat in the window?"
2. Watch it to see if its tail moves, said Peter.
3. It's real! exlaimed Angela when she saw the cat curl its tail.

1. Angela asked, "Is that a real cat or a toy cat in the window?"
2. "Watch it to see if its tail moves," said Peter.
3. "It's real!" exclaimed Angela when she saw the cat curl its tail.

Unit 6 | Week 32 | Day 2

1. "The baseball game sure looks different in person than on television" Felipe said.
2. His sister replied "That's what everyone says."
3. "That's because the television camera shows only a small part of the action at any one time" she explained.

1. "The baseball game sure looks different in person than on television," Felipe said.
2. His sister replied, "That's what everyone says."
3. "That's because the television camera shows only a small part of the action at any one time," she explained.

Unit 6 | Week 32 | Day 3

1. "I grew to twice my size" Carla said as she looked in the funhouse mirror.
2. Jason laughed "That's not really you."
3. "I know because I am looking at the real you" he said.

1. "I grew to twice my size," Carla said as she looked in the funhouse mirror.
2. Jason laughed, "That's not really you."
3. "I know because I am looking at the real you," he said.

Unit 6 | Week 32 | Day 4

1. I'll bet that twig on the ground is really a bug, Tamara said.
2. Michael asked, "how can you tell?"
3. "We'll get close and blow on it very gently to see if it moves" Tamara answered.

1. "I'll bet that twig on the ground is really a bug," Tamara said.
2. Michael asked, "How can you tell?"
3. "We'll get close and blow on it very gently to see if it moves," Tamara answered.

Unit 6 | Week 32 | Day 5

1. Dan said, "it sure looks like Brian is really singing."
2. Susan replied "He's just mouthing the words."
3. Let's find out by turning off the radio, Dan suggested.

1. Dan said, "It sure looks like Brian is really singing."
2. Susan replied, "He's just mouthing the words."
3. "Let's find out by turning off the radio," Dan suggested.

Review Paragraphs for Proofreading

Jamie and her father walked around the muzeum looking for the dinosore dissplay. When they found it, Jamie pointed to a huge skelaton. Look at the size of that! she exclaimed. Did that animal really live on earth? she asked.

Yes, but it lived a long, long time ago, Jamie's father answered. He explained "what you see here are bones that were dug up by scientists. The bones were then put together to restoar the animal to its original size."

Are the plants around the animal real too? Jamie asked.

Her father smiled and said "no, Jamie. You know that real plants need fresh air and sunlight to live."

Jamie nodded and said "let's go see the whales."

Jamie and her father walked around the museum looking for the dinosaur display. When they found it, Jamie pointed to a huge skeleton. "Look at the size of that!" she exclaimed. "Did that animal really live on earth?" she asked.

"Yes, but it lived a long, long time ago," Jamie's father answered. He explained, "What you see here are bones that were dug up by scientists. The bones were then put together to restore the animal to its original size."

"Are the plants around the animal real, too?" Jamie asked.

Her father smiled and said, "No, Jamie. You know that real plants need fresh air and sunlight to live."

Jamie nodded and said, "Let's go see the whales."

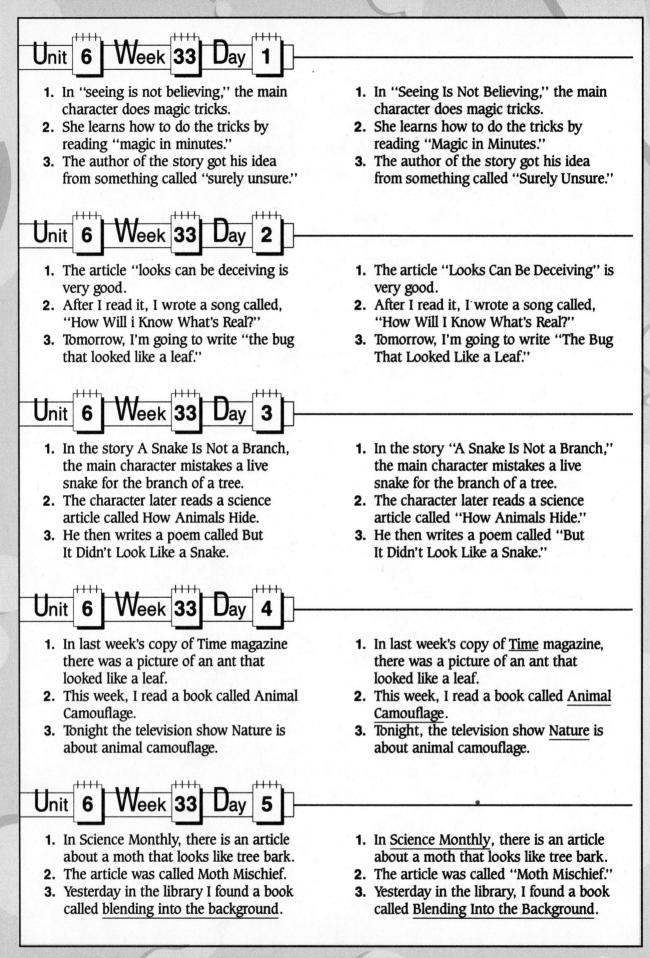

Unit 6 | Week 33 | Day 1

1. In "seeing is not believing," the main character does magic tricks.
2. She learns how to do the tricks by reading "magic in minutes."
3. The author of the story got his idea from something called "surely unsure."

1. In "Seeing Is Not Believing," the main character does magic tricks.
2. She learns how to do the tricks by reading "Magic in Minutes."
3. The author of the story got his idea from something called "Surely Unsure."

Unit 6 | Week 33 | Day 2

1. The article "looks can be deceiving is very good.
2. After I read it, I wrote a song called, "How Will i Know What's Real?"
3. Tomorrow, I'm going to write "the bug that looked like a leaf."

1. The article "Looks Can Be Deceiving" is very good.
2. After I read it, I wrote a song called, "How Will I Know What's Real?"
3. Tomorrow, I'm going to write "The Bug That Looked Like a Leaf."

Unit 6 | Week 33 | Day 3

1. In the story A Snake Is Not a Branch, the main character mistakes a live snake for the branch of a tree.
2. The character later reads a science article called How Animals Hide.
3. He then writes a poem called But It Didn't Look Like a Snake.

1. In the story "A Snake Is Not a Branch," the main character mistakes a live snake for the branch of a tree.
2. The character later reads a science article called "How Animals Hide."
3. He then writes a poem called "But It Didn't Look Like a Snake."

Unit 6 | Week 33 | Day 4

1. In last week's copy of Time magazine there was a picture of an ant that looked like a leaf.
2. This week, I read a book called Animal Camouflage.
3. Tonight the television show Nature is about animal camouflage.

1. In last week's copy of _Time_ magazine, there was a picture of an ant that looked like a leaf.
2. This week, I read a book called _Animal Camouflage_.
3. Tonight, the television show _Nature_ is about animal camouflage.

Unit 6 | Week 33 | Day 5

1. In Science Monthly, there is an article about a moth that looks like tree bark.
2. The article was called Moth Mischief.
3. Yesterday in the library I found a book called blending into the background.

1. In _Science Monthly_, there is an article about a moth that looks like tree bark.
2. The article was called "Moth Mischief."
3. Yesterday in the library, I found a book called _Blending Into the Background_.

REVIEW PARAGRAPHS FOR PROOFREADING

Silvia picked up Science for Students magazine and turned to the page titled ''solve this puzzel and win a fabulous prize.'' On the page Silvia saw six close-up pictures of some very misterious-looking things. All she had to do to win the prize was to tell what was in each picture. ''What a challenge,'' Silvia thought to herself. ''These pictures are a mistery. I'm sure they aren't at all what they seem to be, whatever that is.''

The next day Silvia studied the puzling pictures and sent in her answers. It would take six weeks for the comitte to decide the winner. In the meantime, Silvia wrote an article for her school newspaper, The Trumpet. She called her article Pictures Can Lie.

Silvia picked up <u>Science for Students</u> magazine and turned to the page titled ''Solve This Puzzle and Win a Fabulous Prize.'' On the page, Silvia saw six close-up pictures of some very mysterious-looking things. All she had to do to win the prize was to tell what was in each picture. ''What a challenge,'' Silvia thought to herself. ''These pictures are a mystery. I'm sure they aren't at all what they seem to be, whatever that is.''

The next day, Silvia studied the puzzling pictures and sent in her answers.It would take six weeks for the committee to decide the winner. In the meantime, Silvia wrote an article for her school newspaper, <u>The Trumpet</u>. She called her article ''Pictures Can Lie.''

Unit 6 Week 34 Day 1

1. Please meat me at dawn.
2. Are you sure you want to sea me then.
3. I no I do.

1. Please meet me at dawn.
2. Are you sure you want to see me then?
3. I know I do.

Unit 6 Week 34 Day 2

1. Dew you have the time?
2. The son is sinking in the west.
3. I'm sure your sun is here.

1. Do you have the time?
2. The sun is sinking in the west.
3. I'm sure your son is here.

Unit 6 Week 34 Day 3

1. Can you here me?
2. I can't sea you at all.
3. The too boys looked puzzled.

1. Can you hear me?
2. I can't see you at all.
3. The two boys looked puzzled.

Unit 6 Week 34 Day 4

1. I went two the store.
2. Is one and one too?
3. I am going, two.

1. I went to the store.
2. Is one and one two?
3. I am going, too.

Unit 6 Week 34 Day 5

1. They're is that nasty cat.
2. I won't stand over their.
3. Their not going to the party.

1. There is that nasty cat.
2. I won't stand over there.
3. They're not going to the party.

REVIEW PARAGRAPHS FOR PROOFREADING

''Meat me at seven,'' Sally urged. ''We can go to the new monstre movie in town.''

I had no interest in seaing a movie about an invashun from another planet. Science fiction did not interest me.

''I've already seen to scary movies with you this year. I'm not going and I dont want to argu with you.''

''Please,'' Sally said. ''I have to sea this.'' She was about to bawle. ''They envade the planet and everything. Please come.''

''Okay,'' I said. I don't no how Sally always gets me to do what she wants.

''Meet me at seven,'' Sally urged. ''We can go to the new monster movie in town.''

I had no interest in seeing a movie about an invasion from another planet. Science fiction did not interest me.

''I've already seen two scary movies with you this year. I'm not going, and I don't want to argue with you.''

''Please,'' Sally said. ''I have to see this.'' She was about to bawl. ''They invade the planet and everything. Please come.''

''Okay,'' I said. I don't know how Sally always gets me to do what she wants.

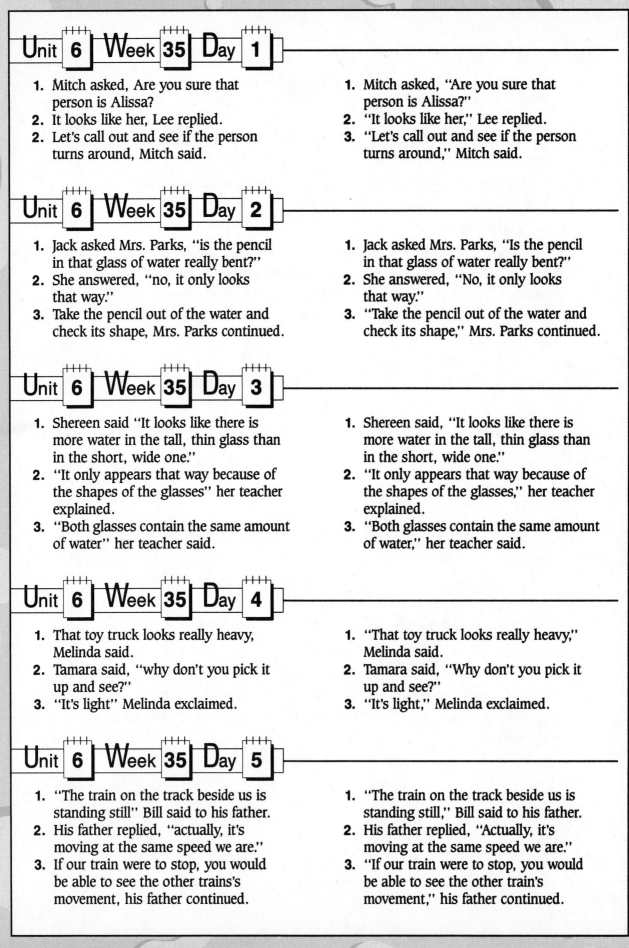

Unit 6 Week 35 Day 1

1. Mitch asked, Are you sure that person is Alissa?
2. It looks like her, Lee replied.
2. Let's call out and see if the person turns around, Mitch said.

1. Mitch asked, "Are you sure that person is Alissa?"
2. "It looks like her," Lee replied.
3. "Let's call out and see if the person turns around," Mitch said.

Unit 6 Week 35 Day 2

1. Jack asked Mrs. Parks, "is the pencil in that glass of water really bent?"
2. She answered, "no, it only looks that way."
3. Take the pencil out of the water and check its shape, Mrs. Parks continued.

1. Jack asked Mrs. Parks, "Is the pencil in that glass of water really bent?"
2. She answered, "No, it only looks that way."
3. "Take the pencil out of the water and check its shape," Mrs. Parks continued.

Unit 6 Week 35 Day 3

1. Shereen said "It looks like there is more water in the tall, thin glass than in the short, wide one."
2. "It only appears that way because of the shapes of the glasses" her teacher explained.
3. "Both glasses contain the same amount of water" her teacher said.

1. Shereen said, "It looks like there is more water in the tall, thin glass than in the short, wide one."
2. "It only appears that way because of the shapes of the glasses," her teacher explained.
3. "Both glasses contain the same amount of water," her teacher said.

Unit 6 Week 35 Day 4

1. That toy truck looks really heavy, Melinda said.
2. Tamara said, "why don't you pick it up and see?"
3. "It's light" Melinda exclaimed.

1. "That toy truck looks really heavy," Melinda said.
2. Tamara said, "Why don't you pick it up and see?"
3. "It's light," Melinda exclaimed.

Unit 6 Week 35 Day 5

1. "The train on the track beside us is standing still" Bill said to his father.
2. His father replied, "actually, it's moving at the same speed we are."
3. If our train were to stop, you would be able to see the other trains's movement, his father continued.

1. "The train on the track beside us is standing still," Bill said to his father.
2. His father replied, "Actually, it's moving at the same speed we are."
3. "If our train were to stop, you would be able to see the other train's movement," his father continued.

REVIEW PARAGRAPHS FOR PROOFREADING

Do you think this rock could really be a piece of bone from a dinosaur skeliton? Dr. Winston asked his partner.

"There's only one way to solve that puzle" Dr. Jones replied. "we'll take it back to the laboratory at the muzeum and have them do tests."

Dr. Winston said eagerly, "let's pack up our gear and get going." He couldn't wait to find out the answer to the puzling mystory.

"Do you think this rock could really be a piece of bone from a dinosaur skeleton?" Dr. Winston asked his partner.

"There's only one way to solve that puzzle," Dr. Jones replied. "We'll take it back to the laboratory at the museum and have them do tests."

Dr. Winston said eagerly, "Let's pack up our gear and get going." He couldn't wait to find out the answer to the puzzling mystery.

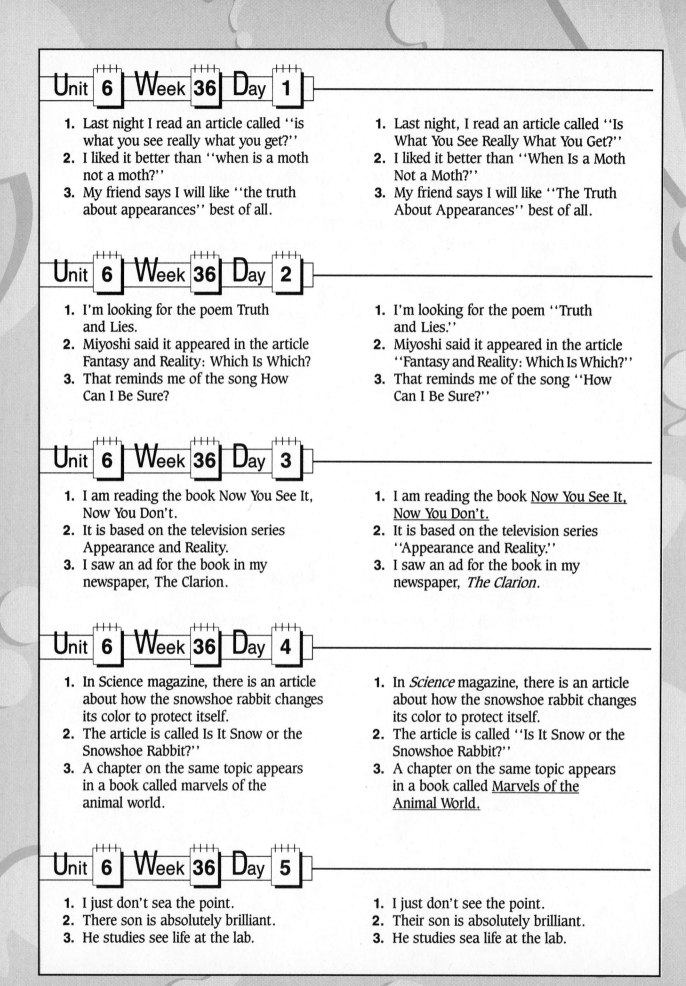

Unit 6 | Week 36 | Day 1

1. Last night I read an article called ''is what you see really what you get?''
2. I liked it better than ''when is a moth not a moth?''
3. My friend says I will like ''the truth about appearances'' best of all.

1. Last night, I read an article called ''Is What You See Really What You Get?''
2. I liked it better than ''When Is a Moth Not a Moth?''
3. My friend says I will like ''The Truth About Appearances'' best of all.

Unit 6 | Week 36 | Day 2

1. I'm looking for the poem Truth and Lies.
2. Miyoshi said it appeared in the article Fantasy and Reality: Which Is Which?
3. That reminds me of the song How Can I Be Sure?

1. I'm looking for the poem ''Truth and Lies.''
2. Miyoshi said it appeared in the article ''Fantasy and Reality: Which Is Which?''
3. That reminds me of the song ''How Can I Be Sure?''

Unit 6 | Week 36 | Day 3

1. I am reading the book Now You See It, Now You Don't.
2. It is based on the television series Appearance and Reality.
3. I saw an ad for the book in my newspaper, The Clarion.

1. I am reading the book <u>Now You See It, Now You Don't.</u>
2. It is based on the television series ''Appearance and Reality.''
3. I saw an ad for the book in my newspaper, *The Clarion*.

Unit 6 | Week 36 | Day 4

1. In Science magazine, there is an article about how the snowshoe rabbit changes its color to protect itself.
2. The article is called Is It Snow or the Snowshoe Rabbit?''
3. A chapter on the same topic appears in a book called marvels of the animal world.

1. In *Science* magazine, there is an article about how the snowshoe rabbit changes its color to protect itself.
2. The article is called ''Is It Snow or the Snowshoe Rabbit?''
3. A chapter on the same topic appears in a book called <u>Marvels of the Animal World.</u>

Unit 6 | Week 36 | Day 5

1. I just don't sea the point.
2. There son is absolutely brilliant.
3. He studies see life at the lab.

1. I just don't see the point.
2. Their son is absolutely brilliant.
3. He studies sea life at the lab.

REVIEW PARAGRAPH FOR PROOFREADING

I am not sure whether I liked the book red sky in wioming better than the book the oregun trail. I enjoy the Far West very much, so I like to read books about it. I have traveled in Navada, Utau, and Montena. I own many books about those states. I have quite a few magazines about the Far West, two.

———

I am not sure whether I liked the book Red Sky in Wyoming better than the book The Oregon Trail. I enjoy the Far West very much, so I like to read books about it. I have traveled in Nevada, Utah, and Montana. I own many books about those states. I have quite a few magazines about the Far West, too.

GRAMMAR, MECHANICS, AND USAGE HANDBOOK AND GLOSSARY

GRAMMAR, MECHANICS, AND USAGE HANDBOOK AND GLOSSARY

The **Grammar, Mechanics, and Usage Handbook and Glossary** that is included in this section of the **Writer's Workshop** contains the following:

- **Punctuation Guide**
  End Punctuation
  Periods
  Commas
  Colons
  Quotation Marks
  Italics (Underlining)
  Apostrophes
  Hyphens

- **Capitalization Guide**
  First Word in Sentences
  Proper Nouns: Names and Titles of People
  Proper Nouns: Names of Places
  Other Proper Nouns and Adjectives

- **Usage Guide**
  Noun Plurals
  Verb Forms
  Adjective Forms

The **Glossary** contains definitions for writing, language, and literary terms. You may wish to duplicate this **Handbook and Glossary** for each of your students and ask them to keep it in their writing folder for easy reference.

This **Grammar, Mechanics, and Usage Handbook** is a good reference for writers. It contains rules about capitalization and punctuation. It also contains some information about verb forms, adjective forms, and noun spellings. You'll find the U.S. Postal Service state abbreviations in this handbook, too.

Punctuation Guide

End Punctuation

Use end punctuation at the end of a sentence.

A **period** ends a declarative sentence. A declarative sentence makes a statement.
John cooks breakfast on Saturday.

A **period** ends an imperative sentence. An imperative sentence makes a command or a request.
Turn right here. (command)   Please close the door. (request)

A **question mark** ends an interrogative sentence. An interrogative sentence asks a question.
How many pencils do you want?

An **exclamation mark** ends an exclamatory sentence. An exclamatory sentence expresses strong emotion.
Sandy won first place!

Periods

Use a **period** at the end of an abbreviation (in informal writing).
Road—Rd.   Boulevard—Blvd.   Mountain—Mt.
Monday—Mon.   September—Sept.
Andrew Morris, Jr. (Junior)   Jan Jones, M.D. (Medical Doctor)

Use a **period** in abbreviations for time (in both formal and informal writing).
9:15 A.M.   12:30 P.M.

Use a **period** after initials.
J. Malloy   Mike C. Cooney

Use a **period** after numerals and letters in outlines.
I. Favorite birds
   A. Blue jay
   B. Eagle

Commas

Use a **comma** between the name of a city and a state in an address.
Monroe, Louisiana   Dallas, TX

Use a **comma** before and after the name of a state or a country when it is used with the name of a city in a sentence.
We visited San Francisco, California, and Honolulu, Hawaii, on our vacation.

Use a **comma** between the day and year in a date.
April 17, 1983

Use a **comma** before and after the year when it is used with both the month and the day in a sentence. Do not use a comma if only the month and the year are given.
I saw her on August 21, 1984, at the park in New Orleans.
I saw her in August 1984 at the park in New Orleans.

Use **commas** to separate three or more items in a series.
Frank likes to eat peaches, pears, and pineapples.

Use a **comma** before *and, but,* or *or* when they join simple sentences to form a compound sentence.
The leaves turn red, and they fall to the ground.

Use a **comma** after the greeting in a friendly letter and after the closing in all letters.
Dear Dad,   Yours,

Use a **comma** to set off a direct quotation.
"What shiny apples," Maggie declared.
"Eddie shines each one," explained Sal, "by hand."

Use a **comma** to set off a noun of direct address.
Juan, your story was excellent.

Use a **comma** to set off the words *yes* and *no* when they begin a sentence.
Yes, I love sports.
No, I do not have a horse.

Colons

Use a **colon** to separate the hour and the minute when you write the time of day.
We will begin the class at 2:15 tomorrow afternoon.

Use a **colon** after the salutation of a business letter.
Dear Sir:

Quotation Marks

Use **quotation marks** before and after a direct quotation, the exact words that a speaker says.

Sam replied, "Go around the corner."

Use a **comma** to separate a phrase such as *he said* from the quotation itself. Place the comma outside the opening quotation marks but inside the closing quotation marks.

"I can't believe," she sighed, "I ran three miles."

Place a **period** inside closing quotation marks.

Miya urged, "Choose the green one."

Place a **question mark** or an **exclamation mark** inside the quotation marks when it is part of the quotation.

He asked, "Don't you like the blue marble?"

Use **quotation marks** around the title of a short story, a song, a short poem, magazine or newspaper article, and a chapter of a book.

Short Story: "The Talking Eggs"
Song: "A Song of Greatness"
Poem: "Imagination"
Magazine Article: "Travel in the Andes"
Newspaper Article: "Science and You"
Book Chapter: "The California Gold Rush"

Italics (Underlining)

Use **italics** or **underlining** to set off the title of a book, movie, magazine, newspaper, or TV series.

Write Idea   *Wizard of Oz*   *Newsweek*   The Super Squad
The New York Times   Growing Pains

Apostrophes

Use an **apostrophe** and an *s* ('s) to form the possessive of a singular noun.

Sally's mittens   the man's thoughts

Use an **apostrophe** and an *s* ('s) to form the possessive of a plural noun that does not end in *s.*

the children's toys   the men's ties

Use an **apostrophe** alone to form the possessive of a plural noun that ends in *s.*

the girls' dresses   the dogs' yelps

Use an **apostrophe** in a contraction to show where letters have been omitted.

we + are = we're   he + is = he's   would + not = wouldn't

Hyphens

Use a **hyphen** to show the division of a word at the end of a line. Divide the word between syllables.

I wanted to go on a very long and restful vacation, but I was not able to do so.

Abbreviations

In both informal and formal writing, you may use abbreviations for certain organizations and government agencies. Such abbreviations usually contain all capital letters and no periods.

World Health Organization (WHO)

In informal writing and on envelopes, you may use United States Postal Service abbreviations for the names of states.

Alabama – AL	Kentucky – KY	Ohio – OH
Alaska – AK	Louisiana – LA	Oklahoma – OK
Arizona – AZ	Maine – ME	Oregon – OR
Arkansas – AR	Maryland – MD	Pennsylvania – PA
California – CA	Massachusetts – MA	Rhode Island – RI
Colorado – CO	Michigan – MI	South Carolina – SC
Connecticut – CT	Minnesota – MN	South Dakota – SD
Delaware – DE	Mississippi – MS	Tennessee – TN
District of	Missouri – MO	Texas – TX
Columbia – DC	Montana – MT	Utah – UT
Florida – FL	Nebraska – NE	Vermont – VT
Georgia – GA	Nevada – NV	Virginia – VA
Hawaii – HI	New Hampshire – NH	Washington – WA
Idaho – ID	New Jersey – NJ	West Virginia – WV
Illinois – IL	New Mexico – NM	Wisconsin – WI
Indiana – IN	New York – NY	Wyoming – WY
Iowa – IA	North Carolina – NC	
Kansas – KS	North Dakota – ND	

In scientific writing, use abbreviations for units of measure. The abbreviation is the same for singular and plural units.

inch—in. pounds—lb kilometer—km liter—L

CAPITALIZATION GUIDE

First Word in Sentences

Capitalize the first word of a sentence.

The capital of Utah is Salt Lake City.

Capitalize the first word of a direct quotation. Do not capitalize the second part of an interrupted quotation unless it begins a new sentence.

Dan cried, "Please stop the presses."

"I am leaving," Jan declared, "as soon as I can."

Capitalize all words in a letter's greeting.

Dear Cousin,

Capitalize the first word in the closing of a letter.

Sincerely yours,

Proper Nouns: Names and Titles of People

Capitalize the names of people and the initials that stand for their names.

Sherri L. Hayek   S. L. Hayek

Capitalize titles of respect or abbreviations of titles when they come before the names of people.

Mr. Marc Jacobs   General B. J. Sutton   Dr. Ellen Stevens

Capitalize words that show family relationships when used as titles or as substitutes for a person's name.

Then Dad and Grandma Bea cooked dinner.

Do not capitalize words that show family relationships when they are preceded by a possessive noun or pronoun.

Sarah's grandmother is very nice.

Her dad is great, too.

Capitalize the pronoun *I*.

Can I go to Jack's house?

Proper Nouns: Names of Places

Capitalize the names of cities, states, countries, and continents.

Camden   Virginia   Mexico   Africa

Capitalize the names of bodies of water and geographical features.
    Red Sea   the Rocky Mountains

Capitalize the names of sections of the country.
    the South   the Pacific Northwest

Do not capitalize words that are used just to show direction.
    Los Angeles is south of San Francisco.

Capitalize the names of streets and highways.
    Huyler Avenue   Highway 107

Capitalize the names of buildings and bridges.
    the National Gallery   Golden Gate Bridge

Capitalize the names of stars and planets.
    North Star   Venus

Capitalize *Earth* when it refers to the planet. Do not capitalize *earth* when preceded by *the*. Do not capitalize *sun* or *moon*.
    From a satellite, Earth looks small.
    The earth is our home.

Other Proper Nouns and Adjectives

Capitalize the names of schools, clubs, and businesses.
    Davis Elementary School   Girl Scouts   General Motors

Capitalize the names of historic events, periods of time, and documents.
    Boston Tea Party   Renaissance   Bill of Rights

Capitalize the days of the week, months of the year, and holidays. Do not capitalize the names of the season.
    Thursday   August   Memorial Day   spring

Capitalize abbreviations.
    Jim Appleton, Jr.   Wed.   Col. Barbara Johnson

Capitalize the first word and all important words in the titles of books, plays, short stories, poems, films, articles, newspapers, magazines, TV series, chapters of books, and songs.

Book, play, short story:	*The Marble Champ, Cats,* "Cinderella"
Poem, movie, article:	"Fog," *Home Alone,* "Cats and You"
Newspaper, magazine:	*Denver Post, People*
TV series, chapter of a book:	*Growing Pains,* "The Southwest,"
Song:	"My Old Kentucky Home"

Capitalize the names of ethnic groups, nationalities, and languages.

> African   Turkish   German

Capitalize proper adjectives that are formed from the names of ethnic groups and nationalities.

> Italian bread   Egyptian cotton

Capitalize the first word of each main topic and subtopic in an outline.

> I. National population
> A. Urban areas
> B. Rural areas

Usage Guide

Forming Noun Plurals

You can use this chart when you want to spell plural nouns. Remember, some plural nouns have irregular spellings. Other plural nouns keep the same spelling as the singular form.

Singular Nouns	To Form Plural	Examples
most singular nouns	add *s*	girl dog hat girls dogs hats
nouns ending with *s, ss, x, z, ch, sh*	add *es*	box watch kiss boxes watches kisses
nouns ending with a consonant and *y*	change the *y* to *i* and add *es*	hobby city sky hobbies cities skies
nouns ending with *ff, f,* or *fe*	most add *s;* some change *f* to *ve;* add *s*	roof life calf roofs lives calves
nouns ending with a vowel and *o*	add *s*	radio studio rodeo radios studios rodeos
nouns ending with a consonant and *o*	generally add *s* but sometimes *es*	piano cello tomato pianos cellos tomatoes

some nouns ending with a consonant and *o*	add either *s* or *es*	volcanos or volcanoes mottos or mottoes
some irregular nouns	change their spelling	tooth foot man teeth feet men
a few irregular nouns	keep the same spelling	moose deer trout

Verb Forms

Irregular verbs do not add *-ed* or *-d* to form the past or past participle.

Verb	Past	Past Participle
be	was	(have, has, or had) been
do	did	(have, has, or had) done
go	went	(have, has, or had) gone
begin	began	(have, has, or had) begun
come	came	(have, has, or had) come
drink	drank	(have, has, or had) drunk
run	ran	(have, has, or had) run
sing	sang	(have, has, or had) sung
swim	swam	(have, has, or had) swum
choose	chose	(have, has, or had) chosen
drive	drove	(have, has, or had) driven
eat	ate	(have, has, or had) eaten
give	gave	(have, has, or had) given
ride	rode	(have, has, or had) ridden
speak	spoke	(have, has, or had) spoken
take	took	(have, has, or had) taken
write	wrote	(have, has, or had) written
draw	drew	(have, has, or had) drawn
grow	grew	(have, has, or had) grown
fly	flew	(have, has, or had) flown
know	knew	(have, has, or had) known
see	saw	(have, has, or had) seen
throw	threw	(have, has, or had) thrown
wear	wore	(have, has, or had) worn
bring	brought	(have, has, or had) brought
teach	taught	(have, has, or had) taught
make	made	(have, has, or had) made
say	said	(have, has, or had) said
sit	sat	(have, has, or had) sat

Adjective Forms

You can use this chart when you need help with comparative and superlative adjective forms. Remember, some adjectives are irregular. They do not form their comparative or superlative forms in the usual way.

Adjective	Compares Two Nouns	Compares More Than Two Nouns
small	smaller	smallest
thin	thinner	thinnest
lengthy	lengthier	lengthiest
tiny	tinier	tiniest
gruesome	more gruesome	most gruesome
active	less active	least active
likable	more likable	most likable
energetic	less energetic	least energetic
much, many	more	most
little	less	least
good	better	best
bad	worse	worst
far	farther	farthest

GLOSSARY OF WRITING, LANGUAGE, AND LITERARY TERMS

This **Glossary** explains writing, language, and literary words and phrases that might be helpful to you in your writing. You might want to keep this **Glossary** in your writing folder.

Writing Terms

audience	the reader or readers for whom something is written
brainstorming	a way to focus a writing topic by writing or listing any thoughts that come to mind about the topic
charting	a way to organize and classify ideas and information by gathering them under different headings—especially useful in comparing and contrasting
checklist	a list of items, such as tasks or topic details, that can be used as an organizer and as a reference source. *See also* **listing**.

chronological order — the arrangement of events in the order in which they occur in time. *See also* **time order.**

clarity — the exactness with which the ideas and purpose of a piece of writing are expressed

clustering — a way to explore ideas by gathering details related to the specific writing topic

coherence — the orderly arrangement of ideas in a piece of writing

compare — to explain how two or more things are alike

conference — a meeting between the writer and a partner or a teacher, or in a group, to ask and answer questions about the writing in progress, with the purpose of improving it

contrast — to explain how two or more things are different

description — a piece of writing that creates a clear and vivid picture of a person, a place, or a thing

detail sentences — sentences that tell more about the main idea of a paragraph

diagram — a visual or graphic presentation of information; often used to organize information during prewriting. A Venn diagram is particularly useful for comparing and contrasting.

drafting — the act of capturing ideas on paper; a stage in the recursive process of writing during which the writer gets his or her basic ideas down on paper

elaboration — a writing strategy in which details and images are added to a piece of writing in order to give the topic fuller treatment

entertaining writing — a piece of writing, often humorous or suspenseful, that amuses, intrigues, diverts, or engages the reader for the particular purpose of entertainment

explanation — a piece of writing that presents the facts about a subject in a clear and logical way, and explains to the reader how and why something occurs

freewriting — a way to generate ideas by simply writing continuously for a specified time, without stopping to elaborate or to correct errors

informative writing	a piece of writing that presents information to a reader in a clear, accurate, complete, and coherent way
instructions	an explanation or a set of directions for how to do something. The steps in a set of instructions are arranged in a logical way so that other people can repeat the activity.
letter	a way to communicate informally or formally with someone in writing. A friendly letter has five parts, each of which gives the person who receives the letter important information, and is personal in nature. A business letter has six parts and is written to an audience often unknown to the writer.
listing	a way to organize your thoughts by writing them down and putting them in order—possibly by numbering them
logical order	an arrangement of ideas in an order that makes sense and is easy for the reader to follow
outline	a way to organize topic-related ideas in the order in which they will be discussed—especially useful in organizing a research report
overall impression	the general idea or feeling expressed in a description
personal narrative	a piece of writing in which the writer tells about something that has happened in his or her life
persuasive writing	writing that encourages an audience to share the writer's beliefs, opinions, or point of view
prewriting	the stage in the writing process in which the writer chooses a topic, explores ideas, gathers information, and organizes his or her material before drafting
prewriting strategies	particular ways of gathering, exploring, planning, and organizing ideas before writing a first draft. *See entries for individual prewriting strategies:* **brainstorming, charting, clustering, freewriting, listing, outline, story chart,** *and* **time line.**

proofreading to review writing in order to correct errors in punctuation, capitalization, spelling, and grammar

publishing to share written work with an audience—for example, by reading it aloud, contributing it to a school paper, or posting it on a bulletin board

purpose the writer's reason for writing—for example, to explain, to entertain, or to persuade

reflective writing a piece of writing in which the writer's personal thoughts, ideas, or feelings become an important part of the form. That form can be a poem, a story, or an essay, for example.

report a piece of writing that provides information about a specific subject. A book review is a kind of report that gives information about a book the writer has read, as well as the writer's opinions about it. A research report summarizes information from many sources about a subject.

revising to improve a draft by adding or taking out information, combining and reordering sentences, adding information, or changing word choice according to the purpose and audience

sensory details in a description, the details that appeal to the reader's five senses—sight, hearing, touch, taste, and smell

story chart a way to gather ideas and details under headings important for the writing of a story—setting, characters, plot, problem/solution, and conclusion, for example

style a writer's use of language and sentence structure to create a particular tone

summary an account that tells the most important ideas in what has been read or observed by the writer. A summary can include information from one source or from multiple sources.

supporting details	facts, examples, or sensory details that give more information about the main idea of a paragraph
time line	a way to organize the events of a narrative in chronological order
time order	the arrangement of events in a composition according to when they occur in time—also called **chronological order.** Some time-order words are *first, next, then,* and *last.*
tone	the feeling or attitude a writer expresses toward the subject of a composition through his or her particular style of writing. For example, a writer's tone may be formal, informal, humorous, or critical.
topic sentence	the sentence that states the main idea of an informative, explanatory, or persuasive paragraph
transition words	words or phrases that may help writers to compare and contrast, such as *on the one hand* and *on the other hand;* also, words that link sentences in a narrative, such as *finally* and *in the meantime*
writing process	the recursive stages involved in writing, which usually include prewriting, writing a draft, revising, proofreading, and publishing
voice	the quality of a piece of writing that makes it distinctively the writer's own

Language Terms

action verb	a word that expresses action She *raced* to the car.
adjective	a word that modifies, or describes, a noun or a pronoun That is a *sweet* cookie.
adjective phrase	a prepositional phrase that modifies, or describes, a noun or a pronoun The dress *of red silk* is gorgeous.
adverb	a word that modifies a verb, an adjective, or another adverb She played *well.*

adverb phrase	a prepositional phrase that modifies, or describes, a verb, an adjective, or an adverb The man stands *near the door.*
antecedent	a word or group of words to which a pronoun refers Stan is a fabulous writer, but *he* needs a good editor.
article	a special adjective—*a, an,* or *the* *The* horse took *an* apple from *a* trainer.
common noun	a noun that names any person, place, or thing The *airplane* landed.
complete predicate	all the words that tell what the subject of a sentence does or is Jerry *grew tomatoes and lettuce.*
complete subject	all the words that tell whom or what the sentence is about *Sally Jacobs* is my best friend.
compound sentence	a sentence that contains two sentences joined by a comma and the word *and, or,* or *but* I sang a song, and she played the piano.
conjunction	a word that joins other words or groups of words in a sentence The friends shopped *and* ate dinner.
direct object	a noun or a pronoun that receives the action of the verb Jane gave a *speech* to the class.
helping verb	a verb that helps the main verb to express action Sarah *was* running fast.
indirect object	a noun or a pronoun that answers the question *to whom? for whom? to what?* or *for what?* after an action verb Bill gave *me* a rose.
linking verb	a verb that connects the subject of a sentence to a noun or an adjective in the predicate Joe *is* a secretary.
noun	a word that names a person, a place, or a thing The *dog* chewed on a *bone* in the *kitchen.*

object of a preposition	a noun or a pronoun that follows the preposition in a prepositional phrase I bought a vase in the *shop*.
object pronoun	a pronoun that is used as the object of a preposition, a direct object, or an indirect object Please give the book to *me*.
possessive noun	a noun that shows ownership The *girl's* father came to the play.
possessive pronoun	a pronoun that shows who or what owns something *Our* dog is a collie.
predicate adjective	an adjective that follows a linking verb and describes the subject The boy is *smart*.
predicate noun	a noun that follows a linking verb and describes the subject Carla was the *president*.
preposition	a word that relates a noun or a pronoun to another word in the sentence She gave me a box *of* cookies.
prepositional phrase	a group of words that begins with a preposition and ends with a noun or a pronoun The glass *on the counter* is mine.
pronoun	a word that takes the place of one or more nouns and the words that go with the nouns *He* lent *me* a quarter.
proper adjective	an adjective formed from a proper noun She bought an *African* basket.
proper noun	a noun that names a particular person, place, or thing The *Pacific Ocean* is immense.
run-on sentence	two or more sentences that have been joined together incorrectly I bought a cake yesterday it was chocolate.
sentence	a group of words that expresses a complete thought John and David wrote a letter to their aunt.

sentence fragment	a group of words that does not express a complete thought Wrote a letter to their aunt.
subject pronoun	a pronoun that is used as the subject of a sentence *He* likes baseball very much.

Literary Terms

alliteration	the repetition of the same first letter or initial consonant sound in a series of words Glen gave Gilda a giant giraffe.
autobiography	the story of a person's life written by that person
biography	the story of a real person's life, written by someone else
characters	the people (or animals) who participate in the action of a story or a play
character sketch	a long description of a character that tries to present a thorough and vivid portrait of the character
concrete poem	a poem whose shape suggests the subject of the poem
dialog	the conversations the characters have in a story or a play
fiction	written work that tells about imaginary characters and events. Works of fiction can include novels, plays, poems, short stories, science fiction, folk and fairy tales, myths, and fables.
figurative language	words used in unusual rather than in exact or expected ways, frequently in poetry. **Simile** and **metaphor** are two common forms of figurative language.
free verse	a poem that sounds like ordinary speech and has no regular rhythm or rhyme
haiku	a poem of three lines and usually 17 syllables, in which the poet often reflects on life or nature
idiom	an expression with a special meaning different from the literal meanings of the individual words that make up the expression—for example, ''Time flies.''

imagery	the use of word pictures—images—in writing, to make a description more vivid through especially precise or colorful language
limerick	an English verse form consisting of five lines that rhyme *a a b b a.* The third and fourth lines have two stresses, and the other lines have three stresses.
lyrics	the words of a song
metaphor	a figure of speech in which a comparison is made without using the word *like* or *as* The field was a green blanket.
meter	the regular pattern of beats in a poem
nonfiction	written work that deals with real situations, people, or events. Nonfiction works include biographies, autobiographies, articles, editorials, and news stories.
personification	a description in which human qualities are given to something that is not human The leaves chased each other across the playground.
plot	the action or sequence of events in a story, a novel, a play, or a narrative poem
proverb	a short, familiar saying that expresses a common truth or a wise observation
repetition	the use of the same word, phrase, or sound more than once, for emphasis or effect, in a piece of writing

rhyme	the repetition of syllables that sound alike, especially at the ends of lines of poetry
	   The wrinkled sea beneath him crawls;
	   He watches from his mountain walls,
	   And like a thunderbolt he falls.

rhythm	a pattern of stressed and unstressed syllables, like a regular musical beat, especially in a poem or a song
	   And hand in hand, on the edge of the sand,
	   They danced by the light of the moon.

setting	the time and place in which the events of a story occur

simile   a figure of speech in which a comparison is made using the word *like* or *as*
> The kite soared like a bird.

stanza   a group of lines in a poem that form a complete unit, like a paragraph in a piece of prose writing

story   a piece of writing that has a sequence of events, or **plot**. People in the story, or **characters**, move the action of the story along. The **setting** is where and when the story takes place.

tall tale   a story in which the characters are larger than life and able to perform extraordinary feats. Exaggeration is used in a tall tale.

tanka   a poem of five lines and usually 31 syllables (5, 7, 5, 7, 7) that frequently expresses the poet's reflections on a subject from life or nature

theme   the main idea or meaning of a complete piece of writing

tone   the total effect of language, word choice, and sentence structure used by a writer to express a certain feeling or attitude toward the subject

WRITING MODELS

MODELS FOR SELF-EVALUATION

The models in this section of the **Writer's Workshop** are provided so that students can compare their written products to a well-developed, annotated model. The information in the **Fast Focus** column will be helpful to students for this comparison. Models are provided for the following:

Visitor's Guide
Speech
How-To Guide
Personal Narrative
Story
Limerick
Business Letter
Character Sketch
Report (Social Studies)
Book Review
Comparison/Contrast Composition
Invitation/Thank-You Note
Friendly Letter/Envelope
Directions to a Place
Form
Announcement
Scene
Biography

You may want to duplicate and distribute the models for students to keep in their writing folders. Or you may want to make the models into overhead transparencies to use for the entire class.

FAST FOCUS

Desert Days and Nights

This writer wanted to describe an unusual place.

My uncle lives just outside a small desert town near the Mexican border. His house is actually on land where they used to mine for silver and gold. The days are usually clear and dry, but it is not as scorching as other nearby towns, because it is quite high up. The nights are cool, too, and sometimes in winter it even snows.

The writer created an overall impression of the desert by including details about the plants and animals.

Although my uncle lives in the desert, he is surrounded by more than just flat sand. There are giant saguaro cactuses, with red fruits and white flowers. These plants reach up to forty feet high, and they are homes to woodpeckers and owls. Almost as tall, century plants stand like spikes pointing into the sky. Mesquite trees grow all around, and the wood is great for barbecues.

Sensory details bring the reader into the picture.

Roadrunners and jackrabbits live near my uncle's house, and sometimes at night I have heard the growl of a mountain lion. But I've never seen one.

Speech

FAST FOCUS

The writer begins on a humorous note.

The writer uses a friendly, conversational tone to reach the audience. Vivid words bring the story to life.

The writer ends with a sincere idea expressed in a lighthearted way.

LADIES AND GENTLEMEN

There are many things I could say about Reynaldo, but since it's his birthday, I guess I should be polite. However, I would like to let you all know how generous he is. In fact, it is because of his amazing generosity that we first met.

Two summers ago, I used to spend a lot of time at the baseball field. I'd play some ball, hang out a while, and then play some more until it was time to go home. One sweltering day, in between games, I was standing in line to buy a soda from the ice-cream man. Let me tell you, I was parched. At last it was my turn, but guess what? I was ten cents short! There was a new kid in line behind me, and he lent me the money. Well, to make a long story short, nearly every day for the rest of that summer this kid pestered me for that lousy dime. We got to know each other pretty well.

So now let's all wish my good friend Reynaldo "Many Happy Returns of the Day." And here's your dime back, buddy!

How-To Guide

FAST FOCUS

An Unusual Vegetable

This writer used the first paragraph to introduce the topic of the guide.

Last year, I amazed my friends when I showed them a cucumber inside a bottle. They all wondered how I had managed to get it in there, as the vegetable was much too big to fit through the bottle's narrow neck. Here's how I did it.

In the middle of May, I planted some cucumber seeds in my garden. It is important to wait until there is no danger of a frost, as it would kill the seeds. I planted the seeds under about a half-inch of soil, about six inches apart from each other, in a spot that gets a lot of sun. Because a cucumber plant is a vine, it will grow up a fence, or it can be tied with string to a stake as it grows. I used an old step ladder, and planted seeds on both sides. When I first sowed the seeds, I used some fertilizer in the soil to make sure that the plants would get enough nutrition. Cucumber plants like a lot of water, so I watered the plants on days when it didn't rain.

The writer wrote the steps in the order in which they were followed, and explained the reason for each step.

Soon the vines had started to grow up the step ladder, and there were small cucumbers starting to form. I chose a perfect one about one inch long, but I did not pick it. I gently slipped the vegetable on its stalk into the narrow mouth of a bottle that I laid on one of the steps. Then I covered it with a newspaper, so that the sun's rays coming through the glass would not burn the cucumber. Several weeks later, when it was fully grown, I cut the stalk and showed my cucumber in a bottle to my baffled friends. I had plenty of other cucumbers to eat, too.

The most important quality of a how-to guide is clarity— how clear the steps are for the reader.

Starting the Week

This writer begins with a very direct glimpse of his personality.

I'm a pretty easygoing sort of person, and it takes a lot to get me upset about things. When I woke up yesterday, I had no idea of what was in store. There was a huge amount of math homework due, but math is my best subject, and I had done the work in no time. I was looking forward to the play rehearsal, too.

I got dressed and ran downstairs in a hurry, because I was expecting my science magazine in the mail. Sure enough, there it was, and Jacob, our golden retriever, brought it to me in his mouth. "Thanks boy," I said, but he wouldn't let go. At last I managed to wrestle it free, but it was in tatters. By that time, my cereal was all soggy.

The writer has organized the narrative in time order.

Things looked better on the school bus, though. Wendy and Denise were showing photos of the class trip to the museum, and everybody was having a good laugh. Then I looked at the pictures. Why hadn't anybody told me I was walking around that museum with red marker all over my face?

At school, the math teacher collected our homework. No wonder it had seemed so easy—I had done the wrong pages! Now I have to do all the right pages by tomorrow.

Humor is used effectively throughout the narrative.

The rest of the morning was fine, except I nearly sprained my jaw trying to eat the snack I had packed in my backpack. It turned out to be a rubber cookie that Wendy had slipped in while I wasn't looking. And then lunch was worse than usual, as hard as that may be to believe.

At last it was time for our play rehearsal. "Break a leg," said Denise. The doctor laughed so hard when I told him the story that I almost kicked him with the plaster cast he had just put on my left foot.

A Narrow Escape

FAST FOCUS

From the tone of the first paragraph, you can tell that this is an adventure story. You can also tell that it is set near the ocean.

The writer has used vivid language and dialog to keep the story moving.

The writer has let the audience feel the same suspense as the characters.

The writer increases the excitement until the climax of the story, right at the end.

The writer wraps up the story in a satisfactory way.

Each wave smashing against the cliffs threw showers of spray up into the air. The two children scrambling across the slippery rocks were soaked through, and the weak morning sun did nothing to warm them. It seemed like hours since they had set out from the sandy bay.

"I can see it now!" shouted Jenny, straining to be heard above the roar of the ocean. She clambered down the steep rock into a shallow pool that was sheltered from the raging sea. Her brother Ben followed.

"Are the flashlights still working?" he asked. Two beams of light pierced the gloom. "Then let's go," said Ben. They waded into the small opening.

Hidden behind a ridge in the wall was a narrow gap. The children squeezed themselves into a tight, twisty passage of rock.

"It's just me," said Jenny. "I dropped my flashlight, and it went out. Give me some light." Ben pointed his beam at the ground. There was Jenny's battered old flashlight, lying in the sand. She stooped down to pick it up. "Hey, what's this?" she exclaimed, picking up something small that was laying on the sand. "It's a gold ring–treasure!" she yelled.

Ben and Jenny rushed on along the passage, finally emerging on the other side. "We made it before high tide," yelled Jenny. "We're lucky, sis." Ben smiled.

Limerick

FAST FOCUS

A limerick is a poem of five lines. Lines one and two rhyme with the last line. The third and fourth lines rhyme with each other.

Museum Madness

All my classmates are in the museum,
But it's locked, so nobody can see 'em.
If I shook him real hard
I might wake up the guard
And then I could go in and free 'em.

Bright Light

There once was a fella so bright,
Who always did everything right.
He wrote and he read,
Had facts in his head,
And his brain gave off a nice light.

FAST FOCUS

*This writer wanted
to write a
persuasive letter to
a popular author.*

Mr. John Cisneros ← INSIDE
Macmillan Publishing Company   ADDRESS
866 Third Avenue
New York, NY 10022

*The writer uses
standard business
letter form. The
six parts are:
heading, inside
address, greeting,
body, closing,
signature.*

Dear Mr. Cisneros:

    I am writing to you on behalf of the upper grades ← BODY
at Whitney Elementary School. In a recent vote held by all of
the 5th- and 6th-grade classes here, you were chosen Author
of the Year. This is an honor that has been awarded by your
readers, not by teachers or other adults. Whitney is not a
small school, and we pride ourselves on our library and our
reading program.

    Our language arts teacher noticed that you are currently on
a lecture tour and will be speaking at Kansas City on June 21,
and Springfield on June 25. I do not want to interfere with your

*The language is
formal and
respectful.*

plans, but the town of Clover is halfway between the two cities,
and I would like to invite you to stop here on your way. The school
would be delighted if you could come and speak on any subject
that you choose.

    We will provide transportation. Also, you have been offered
a free room in the best hotel in town. It's the same room that
Harry Truman stayed in when he passed through Clover in 1947.

*The writer presents
details clearly. She
anticipates some
of her reader's
arguments.*

    Please let me know if you will be able to speak here, so we
can make arrangements for your transportation and stay.

Sincerely yours,   ← CLOSING

Tracy Dell   ← SIGNATURE

Tracy Dell, Librarian
Whitney Elementary School

Character Sketch

FAST FOCUS

This writer begins with an overall impression of her aunt.

Vivid language creates a lifelike picture.

AUNT JEANETTE

Most kids think their parents are too fussy because they have to make their own beds. They never met my Aunt Jeanette! Aunt Jeanette is a small, wiry woman with a "1940s" hairstyle. She has thin lips, and perfect posture. At any time, Aunt Jeanette can be found in her home dusting, arranging, or sweeping. In a flash, she is outside fiddling with the family car making sure it's in tiptop shape. With her perfectly manicured hands she weeds the garden, trims the hedges, and cleans the garage. She's always on the lookout for a missing button, a plant the cat knocked over, or dust on the mantle. Like a cat, she stalks the house on tiptoe.

The Lewis and Clark Expedition

Traveling across a land with no roads and no maps, two young men explored a vast unknown territory. After a period of nearly two-and-a-half years, the young adventurers returned from their eight-thousand-mile journey. The Lewis and Clark Expedition is one of the most exciting stories in United States history.

Thomas Jefferson chose Meriwether Lewis and William Clark to lead an expedition to explore the land west of the Mississippi River. With a party of forty-five men, the two men set sail from St. Louis in May 1804. It was harsh work traveling upstream, and during the bitter winter they stayed with the Mandan Indians in North Dakota. In the spring, Lewis and Clark set off with a Shoshoni guide, a woman named Sacajawea. They continued up the river until it met the Rockies, where Sacajawea's tribe supplied them with horses and guides to cross the mountains.

The explorers struggled hard along the twisting paths, but at last they descended the western foothills. At the Snake River, Nez Perce Indians guided Lewis and Clark with canoes, and in November 1805, they reached the Pacific Ocean. After spending the winter there, they began their return trip.

The members of the expedition had been given up for lost, but they arrived back at St. Louis in September 1806. They brought with them reports about geography, plants, and wildlife of the land they had explored, and glowing descriptions of the many Indian tribes who had helped them on their amazing journey.

Totem Pole

by Diane Hoyt-Goldsmith

The writer summarizes the main story events in the hope of creating interest.

Do people still make totem poles? According to Diane Hoyt-Goldsmith in her nonfiction book *Totem Pole,* they do. The narrator, David, is a young boy who lives in Washington State. David's father, an artist and a woodcarver, is a member of the Tsimshian tribe. His father was raised in Alaska. The book is about David's father's talent for making totem poles.

Totem poles record the legends of the important people in a tribe. David explains all the stages his father goes through in making a totem pole. He describes what each part of the totem pole means, the type of trees he must use, and the time it takes to finish one. After the totem pole is finished, there is a ceremony and feast to celebrate the raising of the totem pole.

The writer concludes with a clearly stated point of view about the book.

This follows the ancient traditions of the Northwest Coast Indian peoples. David and his father perform a traditional dance to show how proud they are of their work.

I recommend this book because it shows the ways in which families pass down traditions and skills to their children. The photographs are colorful and complement the story with pictures of the tribe's celebrations and ceremonial clothing.

Comparison/Contrast Composition

The Eastern Coral Snake and the Scarlet Kingsnake

This writer identifies the topic of the composition in the first paragraph.

In the United States, there are two kinds of snakes that are colored red, black, and yellow. One is the Eastern Coral Snake, the most poisonous of all North American snakes. The other is the Scarlet Kingsnake, which is harmless.

Eastern Coral Snakes are in the same family as the Cobra. They are found along the coastal states from south Texas to Alabama, and from Florida to North Carolina. They live in pine woods or cedar woods, sandhill country, and rocky hillsides.

The writer has noted both the similarities and the differences between two animals that resemble each other.

Coral Snakes usually hunt for lizards and small snakes by moving along under logs, leaves, and dry brush. They are shy, and although their venom is very poisonous, people are rarely bitten by them. The Scarlet Kingsnake is a kind of Milk Snake, and it hunts venomous snakes. Kingsnakes are found throughout the United States, especially in the northern states, and they sometimes look very similar to the poisonous Copperhead. They "mimic" dangerous snakes to protect themselves from predators.

The writer has included enough details to make the report useful.

It is not easy to tell the Eastern Coral Snake and the Scarlet Kingsnake apart. Both grow to between two and four feet. Both have bands of bright red, black, and yellow, but the Coral Snake has a blunt, black snout, while the Kingsnake has a more pointy, red snout. On the Coral Snake, the red and black bands are wide, and separated by narrow yellow bands, while the Kingsnake's color bands are all wide.

The writer has checked the facts for accuracy.

The Scarlet Kingsnake is not dangerous to human beings. It is a constrictor, which squeezes its prey, and it does not have the hollow fangs that the Coral Snake uses to deliver its venom. Like all snake-eating snakes, the Kingsnake is immune to other snakes' venom.

The writer concludes by restating the introduction.

As you can tell, these two kinds of snakes look very similar. If you see one of them, think carefully before getting close. The Scarlet Kingsnake can do you no harm, but the Eastern Coral Snake will bite, and its venom can be lethal.

Invitation

FAST FOCUS

An invitation is written to ask someone to join you at a particular activity or place.

Make sure to include details about the time and place of the activity.

39 Ghost Pony Road ← **HEADING**
Santa Ana, New Mexico 87302
August 15, 1992

Dear Charlene, ← **GREETING**

    At last our new house is fit for guests. To ← **BODY** celebrate, we're going to have a big house-warming party next weekend. I'd love it if you could come. If your cousins are still staying with you, they are welcome, too. I have invited Rosa and Antonio, so it should be great.

    We're going to have a pot-luck dinner, where everyone comes with a different dish. Bring whatever you like, but if you could persuade your mom to make some of her vegetable enchiladas, that would be fantastic.

    The party starts at 3:00 P.M. on Saturday, August 24, and lasts till about 8:00 P.M. If you need directions to the house, call me at 555-3124. Don't forget to bring your swimsuits, as the creek is warm and deep right now.

Your friend, ← **CLOSING**

Linda ← **SIGNATURE**

Thank-You Note

FAST FOCUS

This kind of note is written to thank someone for a gift or kindness.

It is polite to mention the gift or kindness in the note.

548 South Linden Drive ← **HEADING**
Westville, Oregon 97001
February 21, 1992

Dear Grandma, ← **GREETING**

    Thank you so much for the membership to the Westville Zoo that you gave me for my birthday. How did you know that it was something I really wanted? ← **BODY**

    As a member, I can take one other person to the special openings. I hope that you'll be my first guest!

Love, ← **CLOSING**

Paul ← **SIGNATURE**

Friendly Letter

FAST FOCUS

A friendly letter has five parts: heading, greeting, body, closing, signature.

The language used in a friendly letter is like the language friends would use in conversation.

Friendly letters are written to share feelings, ideas, information, or to keep in touch.

263 Manor Drive ← **HEADING**
Austin, Texas 78701
October 11, 1992

Dear Jay, ← **GREETING**

At last I have settled into my new home here in ← **BODY**
Austin. When we left Detroit I thought I'd really hate it, but it isn't bad at all. Of course, I do miss the guys a lot, but I'm starting to make some good friends.

Remember how we used to joke about me riding off on horseback, with a ten-gallon hat perched on my head? Well, it isn't like that at all. Or at least, not in this part of Texas. It's lake country, hilly, with a lot of trees and grass—not like in those cowboy movies. School is OK too, and I know you'd like some of the kids in my class.

Are you still working at the bicycle repair shop on Saturdays? Tell Mr. Summers that everyone here is really impressed with the custom job we did on my bike. Please write soon.

Adios partner, ← **CLOSING**

Vinnie ← **SIGNATURE**

Envelope

Vinnie Timperio
263 Manor Drive
Austin, TX 78701

[stamp]

Jay Kavenski
1691 Lakeshore Boulevard
Detroit, MI 48239

Directions to a Place

FAST FOCUS

Directions should be clear, precise, complete, and accurate.

Use an order that is easy to follow.

Here's how to get to my house from the Eastonville railway station. Follow Station Road up the hill until you reach the Elm Hotel. At the hotel, take a left turn onto Dakota Drive. Stay on Dakota Drive until you cross the bridge, and then take the first right turn onto Apple Lane. Keep going until Apple Lane meets Sunset Road, about a quarter of a mile. Turn right onto Sunset Road. My house is the third one on the left, with a red roof and blue shutters.

FAST FOCUS

Application to the Andover Pet Show

When you fill in a form, print neatly.

Type and Breed of Pet ___Cat, Siamese___

Pet's name and age ___Stan, 4 years___

Owner's full name ___Cheyenne Leacock___

Owner's address ___159 Friendship Ave.___
___Andover, SC 29518___

Telephone number ___(803) 555-1692___

Name of your veterinarian ___Dr. Tsao___

Check that your information is complete and accurate.

Has your pet entered the Andover Show before? ___yes___

If so, when? ___1991___

___Cheyenne Leacock___   ___4/17/92___
Signature of applicant   Date

Applicants under the age of 16 must have a parent or guardian complete this section.

Name of parent or guardian ___Willy Leacock___

Telephone number ___(803) 555-1692___

I have given ___Cheyenne Leacock___ permission to enter a pet in the Andover Pet Show.

___Willy Leacock___   ___4/17/92___
Signature   Date

Announcement

FAST FOCUS

An announcement should inform the reader about what the event is and when and where it will occur.

An announcement should be easy to read.

Sequoyah School
is proud to present

"Dr. Winston's Dream"

a new play written and
performed by members
of the Drama Club

Playing at the Sequoyah
School Auditorium,
Monday June 10 through
Friday June 14
Showtime: 7 P.M.
Admission: $2.50 at the door

Scene

FAST FOCUS

Begin with a list of characters and setting.

Characters are identified by printing their names in capital letters.

The words that characters speak come after the colon.

Stage directions are in parentheses to let actors know that these words are not spoken. Dialog and stage directions indicating a character's actions bring the scene to life.

Cast of Characters:

Danny, a 9-year-old boy
Gloria, his friend, an 11-year-old girl
Dr. Nile, a dentist
Her assistant, a man in his twenties

Setting: The waiting room at a dentist's office.

DANNY: It isn't so bad once you're actually in the chair. It's the waiting that's torture.

GLORIA: No need to worry, Dr. Nile is great. She's never hurt me. I like coming here.

DR. NILE'S VOICE (*from behind the office door*): Boy, it's hard to believe how tough this one is to get out.

DANNY: I'm glad that it isn't me.

(*There is a crash behind the wall.*)

DANNY: Well, how do you explain that?

ASSISTANT'S VOICE: Here, Doctor, try prying it out with this screwdriver.

DR. NILE'S VOICE (*from behind the office door*): No thanks, I'm going to stick with this hammer.

GLORIA (*sounding anxious*): I think she must have changed since I was here last.

DANNY (*looking worried*): I'm getting out of here.

(*The office door opens, and the dentist and her assistant walk out, holding some tools and a broken window shade.*)

DR. NILE: Hi guys! You wouldn't believe the trouble we just had getting this old shade down. Now, who's first?

(*The children look at each other and grin sheepishly.*)

Grandma Moses

One of America's most famous artists never took an art lesson, and did not begin painting until she was 76 years old. Grandma Moses became the most famous painter of primitive art of her time. Her work is known throughout the world, and is loved for its charm, vitality, and compassion.

Grandma Moses was born in upstate New York in 1860. Her real name was Anna Mary. The Robertson family was poor, and at the age of twelve she went to live in another household as a servant. She had a lot of duties, but she enjoyed working. In 1887, she married Thomas Moses, and for the next forty years they farmed together. Even when Thomas died, in 1927, Anna Mary kept the farm going. She was in her seventies when the work became too strenuous for her. But she was not the sort of person who is happy doing nothing, so in 1936 she began painting. She showed her paintings at fairs, alongside her canned fruits and jams, and at the local drugstore. By chance, they were noticed by a traveler from New York City who recognized their importance. He took her work to the city, and in 1939 one of her paintings was shown at the Museum of Modern Art. The next year she had her first one-person show, and in 1941 she won the New York State prize for painting.

As her fame spread, she became known as Grandma Moses. Despite her age, she was very active, and each day she got up early, weeded her flower garden, and painted. She also wrote an autobiography. *Grandma Moses: My Life's History* was published when she was ninety-two years old. Grandma Moses lived to be one hundred years old, and during the last year of her life she completed twenty-five paintings. Her work is in many important museums and collections, including the White House.

WRITING PROMPTS

WRITING PROMPTS

The writing prompts in this section of the **Writer's Workshop** may be used to simulate a test situation. Your students may practice the six types of writing presented in this level. Those six types of writing are the following:

UNIT 1   Descriptive Writing: Visitor's Guide

UNIT 2   Explanatory Writing: How-To Guide

UNIT 3   Entertaining Writing: Story

UNIT 4   Persuasive Writing: Letter

UNIT 5   Informative Writing: Report

UNIT 6   Informative Writing: Comparison/Contrast Composition

Picture prompts are also provided so that students can practice writing in response to a picture cue.

Writing Prompt

Unit 1: Visitor's Guide

In the selection "The Talking Eggs," Blanche takes a walk through the woods and meets a very interesting character. As she visits with the interesting woman she meets, Blanche notices many things about the woods and about the place where the woman lives. Write a description for a classmate of a place you know well which you have observed carefully. As a prewriting technique, you might want to create a cluster in which you list all the details, words, or phrases you can think of about the place. When you revise, you might want to check your description against your cluster to make sure you have not omitted anything.

Unit 2: How-To Guide

<u>Be an Inventor</u> is a book about all sorts of marvelous inventions. In it you learned about why the inventors created their inventions and how they went about making them. Think of a time when you made or created something. Write a how-to guide explaining how you did it. List all the steps in order. Write your how-to guide for someone who is in the fourth grade. As a prewriting technique, you may want to create a flow chart of the steps involved in the process you are explaining. When you revise, close your eyes and visualize all the steps in the process to make sure you do not need to add anything.

Writing Prompt

Unit 3: Story

In the selection "Breaker's Bridge," a character meets a mighty challenge and is rewarded by the emperor. Think of a time when you had to meet a challenge. Perhaps your challenge was at school or in a sports situation. Write a story about your experience. Write the story for someone who does not know about how you met the challenge. As a prewriting technique, you might want to make a story outline that includes setting, characters, plot, problem, and solution. When you revise, you might wish to check your story against your outline to see if you need to add anything.

Unit 4: Letter

<u>Dear Mr. Henshaw</u> tells the story of Leigh Botts through the letters he writes to his favorite author Boyd Henshaw. Leigh discovers a great deal about himself through his letter writing. He discovers the things he cares most about. Think of something you care about, something that is important to you. Perhaps you care about protecting animals or about a longer lunch hour. Write a letter to someone expressing your view on the topic you have chosen. In your letter try to convince the person to think the same way you do about the issue. As a prewriting technique, you might want to make a list of the reasons that you have for feeling the way you do. When you revise, you might want to check your letter against your list to make sure you have your reasons in order of importance.

Writing Prompt

Unit 5: Report

In the book <u>The House of Dies Drear</u>, Thomas investigates the mysteries of a house that was used as a station on the Underground Railroad. The Underground Railroad existed during a particular time in the history of the United States—when runaway slaves were escaping from the South and being helped by abolitionists such as Dies Drear. Think of a time in U.S. history that is of interest to you or that you would like to know more about. Conduct some research on this period and write a report about it. Write your report for a friend. As a prewriting technique, you might want to make an outline. When you revise, you can check your report against the sections in your outline to make sure you have presented your report in a logical order.

Unit 6: Comparison/Contrast Composition

In The News About Dinosaurs, several types of dinosaurs are compared and contrasted. Scientists often compare (identify likenesses) and contrast (identify differences) species as part of their investigations. Think of something you could compare and contrast. It might be something from science or it might be something from another subject area. Write a composition that compares and contrasts the two. Write your composition for your teacher. As a prewriting technique, you might want to make a Venn diagram to classify the likenesses or differences. When you revise, you might want to check your composition against your diagram to make sure you have your likenesses and differences categorized accurately.

Writing Prompt with Picture Cue

Story

Look at this picture. Write a story based on what you see in it. Write your story for a friend. As a prewriting technique, you might want to use a story chart in which you outline setting, characters, events, problem, and solution. When you revise, you might want to close your eyes and visualize the major events in the story. Then look at what you have written to see if you need to elaborate on any of the events.

Writing Prompt with Picture Cue

Description

What do you see in this picture? What kind of place do you think this is? Describe what you see to a classmate. Try to use specific details so that your classmate can see what you see. As a prewriting technique, you might want to create a cluster of sensory details. When you revise, compare your description against your cluster to see if you have omitted any details.

Writing Prompt with Picture Cue

Persuasive Letter

Imagine that this beach is located near where you live. Write a letter to the mayor. In your letter ask the mayor to take some action (you decide) to get this beach cleaned up. As a prewriting technique, you might want to make a list of possible reasons for the mayor to take action. When you revise, you might want to compare your draft to your original list to make sure you have presented the strongest reasons.

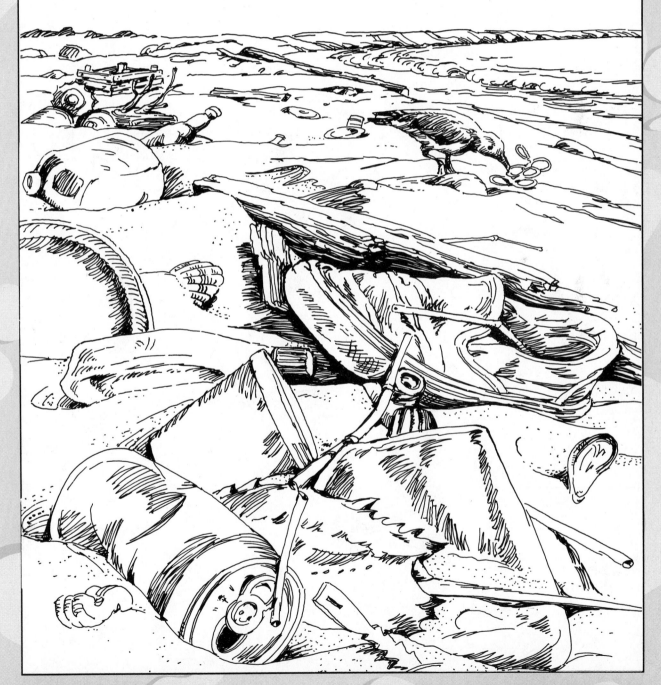

How-to Guide

Look at this picture. Imagine the steps that the cook went through to create the dinner. What materials did he or she need? Write a how-to guide for creating this dinner. Write the guide for someone who is a few years younger than you are. As a prewriting technique, you might want to make a flow chart that lists the steps in order. When you revise, you might want to compare your draft against your flow chart to make sure that your steps are in order.

Writing Prompt with Picture Cue

Comparison/Contrast Composition

Look at this picture. In it are two outfits. How are they alike? How are they different? Write a composition that compares and contrasts these outfits. Write your composition for a relative. As a prewriting technique, you might want to make a Venn diagram to classify likenesses and differences. When you revise, you may want to compare your draft to your diagram to make sure that you have classified your details accurately.

Writing Prompt with Picture Cue

Comparison/Contrast Composition

Look at this picture. There are two creatures from outer space in it. How are they alike? How are they different? Write a composition that compares and contrasts these two creatures. Write your composition for a friend. As a prewriting technique, you might want to make a Venn diagram to show likenesses and differences. When you revise, you may want to compare your draft to your diagram to make sure that you have classified your details accurately.

SPELLING RESOURCES

Spelling Resources

Word Lists at Grade 5

At this level, thirty-six word lists are arranged according to unit. One word list is included for each of the four selections in a unit. Each of these lists contains fifteen words, some of which are from the selection; others contain the same pattern as those words taken from the selection; and others are semantically patterned. A final list, called **Words Worth Knowing**, is a list of thematic or content words related to the unit in some way. There are ten words on these lists since these words are not grouped by pattern and are more difficult. The sixth list is a review list.

Organization of the Spelling Resources

The word lists are divided into sections according to unit. All the word lists for each selection in the unit begin the section. The asterisked words on each list have been taken from the selection. Preceding the list is a seven-step guide for studying spelling words, which is suitable for duplication and intended as a study aid for students to use at home.

Pretests and posttests are provided for each word list. Pretest sentences may be administered before each word list is introduced. The selection spelling words appear in italics in these pretest sentences. After students self-correct their pretests, they may use one of the several spelling activities on page T168. (If you prefer a more structured spelling lesson, you may want to use the **Spelling Activity Pad**, which accompanies this program.)

After students have completed work with the selection words, the posttest may be administered. The selection spelling words appear in italics in these posttest sentences.

Sample test sentences are also included for the cumulative review tests that are provided for each unit; these reviews always contain three words from the **Words Worth Knowing** list.

Other Materials

Also included in the **Spelling Resources** section are individual and class record forms. The **Personal Spelling List** form, which may be duplicated, also appears here. A **How to Study Spelling Chart/Spelling Reminders** page, which lists pertinent tips, strategies, and generalizations, and a cumulative word list for this level are also included. Finally, a list of words most often misspelled is provided.

Spelling as Part of an Integrated Reading/Language Arts Curriculum
by Charles Temple

Stages of Spelling Development

The challenges of spelling change as students progress through the grades. These changes occur for several reasons. First, learning to spell is not a matter of just memorizing words but of forming and revising concepts about spelling structures. Second, students' concepts about and strategies for spelling change as they get older. Finally, the words students encounter at each successive grade level change in their structure.

The following stages of spelling development have been identified in recent research.

Prephonemic At this stage, students write squiggles that resemble writing; the squiggles exhibit no apparent relationship between graphemes and phonemes.

I went fishing.   =   2nxkoop

Prephonemic spelling is common in preschool through mid-first grade (and later, with some students).

Early Phonemic At this stage, students begin to use letters to stand for some sounds in their messages; the message is notably incomplete.

I went fishing.   =   IYTFH

Early phonemic spelling is common in kindergarten and early first-grade students.

Letter Name At this stage, students represent sounds in their messages on the basis of the similarity of the target phonemes and the names of the letters that spell them.

I went fishing.   =   I YET FEHEG

Letter-name spelling is common in students in first and early second grade.

Common Patterns At this stage, students' spellings begin to seem reasonable. Digraphs and long and short vowels are represented, as spelling moves beyond strings of matches between individual sounds and individual patterns. Words at this stage are easily readable, if incorrect.

I went fishing.   =   I WINT FISHING

Common patterns begin to emerge by mid-first grade and may characterize students' spelling from then on.

Derivational Spelling At this stage, students' spelling honors not only common spelling patterns but also common root words.

Not sail/saler   *but* sail/sailor
Not sine/cignal   *but* sign/signal
Not photagraphy/photagraph *but* photography/photograph

Derivational spelling normally begins to show up in students (and in spelling lists) by fourth grade; it comes into serious play in sixth grade and beyond. Many children never develop much of an awareness of derivational spelling, perhaps because an emphasis on spelling instruction often ends before this level of issues is reached.

Since there are progressive changes in the difficulties students have as they move through these stages of development, the teaching strategies that can help them must change as well. Teaching activities need to be varied according to stage, and you will need to be aware of the types of errors that students produce at each stage.

Word Lists in This Program

The literature selections in the reading/language arts program were used as a source of words for 16 of the 20 word lists in this section of the **Writer's Workshop.** The literature selections were first read for words that seemed suitable. Once this list of seemingly suitable words was established, the following procedures were employed:

- The list of suitable words was compared with these sources for grade-level appropriateness:
  - six major basal spelling series
  - *3,000 Instant Words* by Elizabeth Sakiey and Edward Fry
  - *Basic Elementary Reading Vocabularies* by Albert Harris and Milton Jacobson
  - *Computational Analysis of Present Day American English* by Henry Kucera and Nelson Francis
  - *New Iowa Spelling Scale* by Bradley Loomer

- For utility, the list of suitable words was compared with this source:
  - *A Writing Vocabulary for Elementary Children* by Robert Hillerich

- For common spelling patterns, the list of suitable words was compared with these sources:
  - *American English Spelling* by D. W. Cummings
  - *Teaching Spelling* by Edmund Henderson
  - *The Beginnings of Writing* by Charles Temple et al.

Words from the selection that passed all of the above criteria—grade-level appropriateness, utility, and degree of common spelling pattern—were retained. Other words that were grade-appropriate, had high utility, and shared a spelling or semantic pattern with those words from the literature were then added to complete each 15-word list.

In addition, other useful word lists are provided in the program. Such lists include thematically related or content-related words, or words often confused.

Conclusion

All would agree that the ability to spell is secondary to the ability to make meaning. All would also agree, however, that a student's inability to spell (or to see the relationship between sound and symbol) can interfere with making meaning as he or she attempts to decode or to write ideas on paper. Spelling, then, is best taught within the context of reading and writing, both informally—through proofreading experiences with writing that is meaningful to a particular student—and systematically—through word lists of useful, patterned, and developmentally appropriate words derived from familiar texts.

Bibliography

Bryant, Peter, and Bradley, Lynnette. *Children's Reading Problems.* New York: Oxford University Press, 1985.

Buchanan, Ethel. *Spelling for Whole Language Classrooms.* Winnipeg, Manitoba: Whole Language Consultants, 1989.

Cummings, D. W. *American English Spelling.* Baltimore: Johns Hopkins University Press, 1988.

Classroom Practices and Developmental Spelling Stages

As beginning spellers write, they should be encouraged to spell words the way they think they are spelled—not pausing to look up correct spellings and especially not limiting themselves to writing the words they already know how to spell correctly. Students should be encouraged to correct their papers for spelling after they have written the draft and before they share it with others. How do we encourage these practices?

To encourage beginners to invent spellings, you can do a brainstorming demonstration on the board or on a transparency. Begin by calling out a word such as *fishing*. Pronounce the word slowly, and ask students what sound they hear first. Then ask what letter you could write to stand for that sound. Write the letter that is suggested, and go on to the next sound, proceeding until the word is spelled. Note that the emphasis here is not on correctness; the spelling offered by the students may very well be something like *feheg*. The goal is to encourage the practice of invented spelling. If a student asks if the spelling is *right,* you can explain that this is the way that children can spell this word.

Beginning writers use some words over and over. Words such as *is, was, the,* and *this* can be written on post-its and put in the Writing Center or on the wall or door, so that students can refer to them without consulting you. You can also help each student prepare his or her own dictionary of frequently used words. This list need not contain more than fifteen or twenty of the highest-frequency words.

From second grade on, you may wish to demonstrate proofreading for spelling by using a transparency made from actual student work or from your own teacher-created materials. Students can look for misspelled words and supply the correct spelling. If there is doubt, students can be sent to the dictionary. Once the idea of proofreading for spelling has been introduced, students can proofread for spelling in a variety of ways. They may team up with partners, or you may appoint a rotating spelling committee to which students take their papers before publication.

The Value of Word Lists

Are word lists valuable? Is the systematic teaching of spelling from such word lists relevant? Teachers in some classrooms have observed that traditional spelling lists are often irrelevant; the words on those lists disregard students' reading or writing needs. These teachers may elect to teach spelling in a more informal fashion, mainly by cultivating the habits of proofreading.

Other teachers have decided that the weekly, systematic teaching of spelling words is necessary if most students are to learn a large corpus of words that they can spell correctly without having to take the time to look them up. These teachers seek to teach children lists of words on a regular (usually weekly) basis, but they draw these words from those that students often use and misspell or from the literature that students are reading. The advantages of this approach are that students do learn many spelling words, they learn words that are useful to them, and the words they learn are frequently put into practice. A disadvantage, when compared with traditional spelling approaches, is that words chosen topically may not be grouped by patterns—and students may miss the opportunity to learn the patterns of English spelling that would give them control over many more words than those they studied directly.

Is there a rationale that could possibly provide teachers with the "best of both worlds" with regard to relevance and a systematic spelling approach? We think so.

Gentry, Richard. *SPEL is a Four Letter Word.* Portsmouth, NH: Heinemann, 1988.

Harris, Albert J., and Jacobson, Milton D. *Basic Elementary Reading Vocabularies.* New York: The Macmillan Company, 1982.

Henderson, Edmund. *Teaching Spelling, Second Edition.* Boston: Houghton Mifflin, 1990.

Hillerich, Robert. *A Writing Vocabulary for Elementary Children.* Springfield, IL: Charles C. Thomas, 1987.

Kucera, Henry, and Francis, Nelson. *Computational Analysis of Present Day American English.* Providence, RI: Brown University Press, 1967.

Loomer, Bradley. *New Iowa Spelling Scale.* Iowa City: Useful Curriculum Corporation, 1987.

Sakiey, Elizabeth, and Fry, Edward. *3,000 Instant Words.* Providence, RI: Jamestown Publishers, 1984.

Skeat, Walter. *Concise Etymological Dictionary of the English Language.* New York: Oxford University Press, 1984.

Temple, Charles, et al. *The Beginnings of Writing.* Needham Heights, MA: Allyn and Bacon, 1988.

How to Study Spelling Words

Step *1*	Look at the word as your teacher or a friend reads or says it aloud.
Step *2*	Say the word aloud to yourself.
Step *3*	Write the word. Name each letter as you write it.
Step *4*	Say the word again.
Step *5*	Check to make sure you spelled the word correctly.
Step *6*	Cover the word and write it again. Name each letter as you write it.
Step *7*	Check to make sure you spelled the word correctly. If you did not, erase the word. Repeat steps 6 and 7.

Word Lists for Unit 1:

Unforgettable Places

The Wreck of the "Zephyr"
sort
port*
order
border
prove*
who've
who's
who'd
whose
final
surprise
rise
wise
sailor*
fail

The Talking Eggs
narrow*
sparrow
wheelbarrow
mutter
sputter
even
evening*
fold
scold
folk tale
yolk
temper
emptiness
iron*
jewel

The Voyage of the "Dawn Treader"
pleasure
treasure
precious*
delicious
cushion
shiver
manage
image
imagine*
adventure*
mixture
furniture
return
private
wonderful

Dive to the Coral Reefs
surface*
palace
furnace
discover
recover
allow
swallow
disturb
turbulent
ancient*
modern*
explore*
enormous*
legend
tropic

Words Worth Knowing
United States
Mexico
Puerto Rico
Jamaica
Canada
England
Spain
France
Japan
Russia

Review
order
border
who've
United States
Mexico
evening
folk tale
pleasure
treasure
private
wonderful
disturb
ancient
Canada
explore

Pretest Sentences

When to Pretest: Before you introduce each word list you choose to use to accompany this unit, use the appropriate group of sentences below to administer a pretest for the spelling words on that list. After students self-correct their pretests, assign one of the spelling activities provided for practice with spelling strategies.

Directions for Pretesting: Give the spelling word. Read the sentence. Repeat the spelling word. After all the spelling words are given, reread the words so that students can check their spelling.

Scoring: Score one point for each correct spelling word. Have students enter their scores on the **Student Record.**

The Wreck of the "Zephyr"
1. That is some *sort* of tree.
2. Many ships visit the *port.*
3. We obeyed his *order.*
4. They crossed the *border* at night.
5. You cannot *prove* an opinion.
6. *Who've* you brought with you?
7. *Who's* your friend?
8. *Who'd* like to be president?
9. *Whose* book report is this?
10. Is that your *final* answer?
11. I have a *surprise* for you.
12. Bread dough will *rise* slowly.
13. The king had *wise* advisors.
14. The *sailor* is on her boat.
15. I *fail* to see your point.

The Talking Eggs
1. We had a *narrow* escape.
2. The *sparrow* ate a worm.
3. She pushed the *wheelbarrow.*
4. I heard them *mutter* quietly.
5. The angry children *sputter.*
6. They weren't *even* listening.
7. I saw her this *evening.*
8. Help me *fold* these sheets.
9. People *scold* naughty children.
10. I enjoyed the Chinese *folk tale.*
11. The egg *yolk* broke.
12. Why did you lose your *temper?*
13. I felt great *emptiness.*
14. We painted the *iron* fence.
15. A diamond is a *jewel.*

The Voyage of the "Dawn Treader"
1. Reading is a *pleasure*.
2. The king hid his *treasure*.
3. That is a *precious* possession.
4. The apple pie was *delicious*.
5. The bench had a *cushion*.
6. They *shiver* in the winter.
7. We *manage* to fall asleep.
8. That is an *image* of the queen.
9. I can't *imagine* where he is.
10. The pioneers loved *adventure*.
11. Make a *mixture* of milk and tea.
12. The truck delivered *furniture*.
13. When will they *return*?
14. She hired a *private* detective.
15. What a *wonderful* idea!

Words Worth Knowing
1. Texas is in the *United States*.
2. They traveled to *Mexico*.
3. *Puerto Rico* once belonged to Spain.
4. *Jamaica* is a beautiful country.
5. Do you live in *Canada*?
6. My family came from *England*.
7. Columbus sailed from *Spain*.
8. Would you like to go to *France*?
9. The visitors came from *Japan*.
10. *Russia* has many ancient cities.

Dive to the Coral Reefs
1. Fish swim beneath the *surface*.
2. That was the royal *palace*.
3. The *furnace* warms our house.
4. Who really did *discover* that?
5. He will *recover* from the cold.
6. This hotel does not *allow* pets.
7. I will *swallow* my vitamin.
8. Do not *disturb* my notes.
9. They lived in *turbulent* times.
10. *Ancient* Egypt was powerful.
11. Solar cars are a *modern* idea.
12. They *explore* the jungle.
13. Elephants are *enormous* animals.
14. *Rip Van Winkle* is a *legend*.
15. Hawaii has a *tropic* atmosphere.

Review
1. The florist took my *order*.
2. No guards were at the *border*.
3. *Who've* they put in your class?
4. The *United States* is huge.
5. I visited *Mexico* last year.
6. Fireflies appear in the *evening*.
7. The *folk tale* was about a giant.
8. It's a *pleasure* to be here.
9. They are searching for *treasure*.
10. The patient had a *private* room.
11. It was a *wonderful* movie.
12. Don't *disturb* the dog.
13. Did you study *ancient* history?
14. Is *Canada* our neighbor?
15. Shall we *explore* the woods?

Posttest Sentences

When to Posttest: After students have completed work on each word list you use to accompany this unit, use the appropriate group of sentences below to administer the posttest. After students self-correct their posttests, have them record in their **Journals** or on their **Personal Spelling Lists** the words they misspelled.

Directions for Posttesting: Give the spelling word. Read the sentence. Repeat the spelling word. After the spelling words are given, reread the words so that students can check their spelling.

Scoring: Score one point for each correct spelling word. Have students enter their scores on the **Student Record.**

The Wreck of the "Zephyr"

1. It is a *sort* of cat.
2. He unloads boats in the *port*.
3. Do not disobey my *order*.
4. That *border* separates two states.
5. He did not *prove* your guilt.
6. *Who've* you found to help?
7. *Who's* going with me?
8. *Who'd* like to eat?
9. *Whose* bike is out front?
10. This is your *final* warning.
11. Your call was a *surprise*.
12. When will the sun *rise*?
13. The old woman was very *wise*.
14. The *sailor* swam to shore.
15. They *fail* every test.

The Talking Eggs

1. We can't drive on *narrow* streets.
2. The *sparrow* flew away.
3. Is the *wheelbarrow* broken?
4. They *mutter* about getting even.
5. Candles *sputter* and go out.
6. That isn't *even* funny.
7. You can meet her this *evening*.
8. Can you *fold* the paper?
9. We *scold* the barking dog.
10. That is an Irish *folk tale*.
11. The egg *yolk* was hard.
12. He has a terrible *temper*.
13. The *emptiness* was overwhelming.
14. The *iron* pipe is heavy.
15. There was a *jewel* in her ring.

The Voyage of the "Dawn Treader"
1. Her singing gives me *pleasure*.
2. Where is the *treasure* hidden?
3. Children are *precious* to me.
4. She makes *delicious* soup.
5. She sat on a velvet *cushion*.
6. We *shiver* with fear.
7. They *manage* to find help.
8. His *image* is on that stamp.
9. They *imagine* weird stories.
10. Our vacation was an *adventure*.
11. The oil *mixture* caught fire.
12. She sold all of her *furniture*.
13. He didn't *return* to class.
14. The mansion is a *private* home.
15. He brought us *wonderful* news.

Words Worth Knowing
1. The *United States* is home.
2. The Aztecs lived in *Mexico*.
3. *Puerto Rico* is close by.
4. *Jamaica* has a tropical climate.
5. How far are we from *Canada*?
6. My sweater came from *England*.
7. What is the capital of *Spain*?
8. *France* is famous for fashion.
9. They went to *Japan*.
10. Does *Russia* have cold winters?

Dive to the Coral Reefs
1. The table had a wooden *surface*.
2. The *palace* had high gates.
3. She put coal in the *furnace*.
4. When did you *discover* the truth?
5. Did they *recover* their money?
6. Will you *allow* me to help?
7. It hurts when I *swallow*.
8. Phone calls *disturb* my work.
9. The ocean was *turbulent*.
10. Rome is an *ancient* city.
11. We live in the *modern* world.
12. They *explore* the haunted house.
13. The blimp was *enormous*.
14. He told us a Japanese *legend*.
15. He lives in a *tropic* climate.

Review
1. She gave the *order* to begin.
2. We have a *border* with Mexico.
3. *Who've* they elected president?
4. I live in the *United States*.
5. *Mexico* is our neighbor.
6. It is hot this *evening*.
7. We read another *folk tale*.
8. Cooking is a *pleasure*.
9. The queen had a great *treasure*.
10. May I speak to you in *private*?
11. I have a *wonderful* surprise.
12. Tapes *disturb* my studying.
13. Caesar was an *ancient* Roman.
14. *Canada* is a beautiful country.
15. They *explore* the cave.

TRANSFORMATIONS

**New Providence: A
Changing Cityscape**
local
location*
condition*
government*
govern
cruise
bruise
cigarette*
cigar
tribe
tribal
arch
architect*
apartment
advertisement*

The Shimmershine Queens
position*
opposite*
deposit
whisper
whimper
imitation
imitate
perform
performance*
celebrate
celebration
freedom*
powerful*
movement
defeat*

Be an Inventor
produce
reduce
capitol
capital*
expect
respect
inspect
fortune
fortunate*
create
creative
inform
information*
invent
invention*

Words Worth Knowing
California
New Mexico
Arizona
Texas
Oklahoma
New York
Pennsylvania
New Jersey
Delaware
Connecticut

The Gold Coin
instant
constant
distant
guide
guilt
guess
guitar
notice*
noticeable
cupboard*
shepherd
pale
sneaking
shriveled
twisted*

Review
location
information
guide
guilt
Texas
whisper
notice
opposite
celebrate
Oklahoma
position
Pennsylvania
produce
invent
architect

Pretest Sentences

When to Pretest: Before you introduce each word list you choose to use to accompany this unit, use the appropriate group of sentences below to administer a pretest for the spelling words on that list. After students self-correct their pretests, assign one of the spelling activities provided for practice with spelling strategies.

Directions for Pretesting: Give the spelling word. Read the sentence. Repeat the spelling word. After all the spelling words are given, reread the words so that students can check their spelling.

Scoring: Score one point for each correct spelling word. Have students enter their scores on the **Student Record.**

New Providence: A Changing Cityscape

1. She is a *local* hero.
2. I told him our *location*.
3. That *condition* is unacceptable.
4. Our *government* passes laws.
5. They *govern* our state wisely.
6. We *cruise* on the river.
7. My *bruise* was sore.
8. Do not light a *cigarette*.
9. He smoked a *cigar*.
10. Does she belong to that *tribe?*
11. They run the *tribal* government.
12. They built an *arch*.
13. He is a famous *architect*.
14. We need a bigger *apartment*.
15. Give me the *advertisement*.

Be an Inventor

1. What does this factory *produce?*
2. We hope to *reduce* its size.
3. The *capitol* has many rooms.
4. That city is our *capital*.
5. Don't *expect* an answer soon.
6. Show *respect* for others.
7. They *inspect* the clothing.
8. The gold is worth a *fortune*.
9. We were *fortunate* to see you.
10. Blue and red *create* purple.
11. The writer was very *creative*.
12. They *inform* us regularly.
13. We need more *information*.
14. Did you *invent* this machine?
15. I saw her new *invention*.

The Gold Coin
1. I can be there in an *instant*.
2. They lived in *constant* fear.
3. She traveled to *distant* places.
4. We paid our *guide* for the tour.
5. Did he feel any *guilt*?
6. Can you *guess* her age?
7. Max practices on his *guitar*.
8. They *notice* every change.
9. Your bruise isn't *noticeable*.
10. Canned food is in the *cupboard*.
11. The wolf growled at the *shepherd*.
12. He looked tired and *pale*.
13. They were *sneaking* past me.
14. The mummy was *shriveled* and dry.
15. He *twisted* his head to look.

Words Worth Knowing
1. This fruit comes from *California*.
2. She sells jewelry in *New Mexico*.
3. His mom lives in *Arizona*.
4. Austin is the capital of *Texas*.
5. Will Rogers came from *Oklahoma*.
6. That President lived in *New York*.
7. *Pennsylvania* is the Keystone State.
8. They used to live in *New Jersey*.
9. His factory is in *Delaware*.
10. He visited *Connecticut* last week.

The Shimmershine Queens
1. The players are in *position*.
2. We stood on *opposite* sides.
3. The bank took my *deposit*.
4. They *whisper* all the time.
5. You *whimper* in your sleep.
6. That is an *imitation* jewel.
7. She can *imitate* a dog barking.
8. We *perform* plays each week.
9. We applauded their *performance*.
10. We *celebrate* every week.
11. What a great *celebration*.
12. We have *freedom* of speech.
13. She is a *powerful* leader.
14. They joined a new *movement*.
15. We *defeat* our enemies.

Review
1. What is your *location*?
2. I called for *information*.
3. We listened to our *guide*.
4. Do you feel any *guilt*?
5. I took a trip to *Texas*.
6. We like to *whisper* secrets.
7. Did you *notice* the new rug?
8. We had *opposite* opinions.
9. Her parties *celebrate* holidays.
10. *Oklahoma* is west of Illinois.
11. I am in a difficult *position*.
12. Have you been to *Pennsylvania*?
13. These farms *produce* wheat.
14. They *invent* computer programs.
15. My sister is an *architect*.

Posttest Sentences

When to Posttest: After students have completed work on each word list you use to accompany this unit, use the appropriate group of sentences below to administer the posttest. After students self-correct their posttests, have them record in their **Journals** or on their **Personal Spelling Lists** the words they misspelled.

Directions for Posttesting: Give the spelling word. Read the sentence. Repeat the spelling word. After the spelling words are given, reread the words so that students can check their spelling.

Scoring: Score one point for each correct spelling word. Have students enter their scores on the **Student Record.**

New Providence: A Changing Cityscape
1. This is a *local* phone call.
2. Do you know the wreck's *location?*
3. Did you *condition* your hair?
4. He is the head of our *government.*
5. Does Congress *govern* us?
6. The cabs *cruise* all day.
7. There was a *bruise* on his arm.
8. Put out that *cigarette!*
9. He always carried a *cigar.*
10. The *tribe* hunts for food.
11. They showed *tribal* crafts.
12. They toured the *arch.*
13. The *architect* designed a house.
14. I hope to rent an *apartment.*
15. The *advertisement* was great.

Be an Inventor
1. Cars *produce* air pollution.
2. *Reduce* your report to one page.
3. We toured the *capitol* building.
4. London is Britain's *capital.*
5. We *expect* to see him soon.
6. She must *respect* her wishes.
7. The officers *inspect* the army.
8. He made a *fortune* in business.
9. The children felt *fortunate.*
10. They *create* beautiful music.
11. She has a *creative* mind.
12. I will *inform* my parents.
13. The police gathered *information.*
14. Let's *invent* a new game.
15. This recipe is my own *invention.*

The Gold Coin
1. This will be over in an *instant*.
2. They were *constant* companions.
3. They live in a *distant* land.
4. We met our *guide* at the hotel.
5. Her *guilt* made her feel awful.
6. *Guess* who I saw!
7. He plays a *guitar* and sings.
8. Did they *notice* your clothes?
9. These stains are *noticeable*.
10. Put the food in the *cupboard*.
11. The *shepherd* leads the sheep.
12. He wore a *pale* gray suit.
13. They are *sneaking* out of class.
14. The balloon looked *shriveled*.
15. He *twisted* the rope into a knot.

Words Worth Knowing
1. I'd like to visit *California*.
2. He writes stories about *New Mexico*.
3. The sheriff came from *Arizona*.
4. They raise cattle in *Texas*.
5. Tulsa is in *Oklahoma*.
6. The Hudson River is in *New York*.
7. Franklin lived in *Pennsylvania*.
8. Was *New Jersey* an original colony?
9. The Blue Hen State is *Delaware*.
10. They moved to *Connecticut*.

The Shimmershine Queens
1. What *position* do you play?
2. Big is the *opposite* of small.
3. The store returned my *deposit*.
4. We had to *whisper* to each other.
5. I heard the baby *whimper*.
6. This is *imitation* leather.
7. He can *imitate* others very well.
8. They *perform* plays at school.
9. It was her last *performance*.
10. Let's *celebrate* today.
11. We had a holiday *celebration*.
12. People need *freedom*.
13. The machine is very *powerful*.
14. The pioneers loved *movement*.
15. Our armies *defeat* them.

Review
1. That is a great *location*.
2. I will ask for *information*.
3. The *guide* spoke English.
4. Her *guilt* bothered her.
5. We went to *Texas* in April.
6. Did she *whisper* the answer?
7. I did not *notice* the mistake.
8. The tree is *opposite* our house.
9. They *celebrate* their victory.
10. Does *Oklahoma* produce oil?
11. His *position* is in the center.
12. Is *Pennsylvania* near here?
13. Our state did *produce* oil.
14. They *invent* movie ideas.
15. He studied to be an *architect*.

AGAINST THE ODDS

"The Marble Champ"
contest*
protest
target*
marble*
include
exclude
budge*
budget
blast
plastic
champion*
example
figure*
regular
trophy*

"Breaker's Bridge"
whenever
whatever*
possibility
impossible*
guard*
guardian
crouch
pouch*
object
project*
grind
remind
recall
refresh
ache

How It Feels to Fight for Your Life
program*
progress
pressure*
emergency*
urgent
suppose*
propose
type*
typical
collect
collection*
selection
amazing*
flavor*
treatment*

Tonweya and the Eagles
medical
medicine*
connect
connection
suggestion
attention*
royal
protection*
represent*
present
direction*
election
forward*
title*
different*

Words Worth Knowing
Vermont
New Hampshire
Maine
Rhode Island
Massachusetts
Maryland
Virginia
West Virginia
Kentucky
Tennessee

Review
direction
different
medicine
suggestion
emergency
Massachusetts
suppose
Virginia
ache
blast
impossible
Kentucky
figure
champion
connect

Pretest Sentences

When to Pretest: Before you introduce each word list you choose to use to accompany this unit, use the appropriate group of sentences below to administer a pretest for the spelling words on that list. After students self-correct their pretests, assign one of the spelling activities provided for practice with spelling strategies.

Directions for Pretesting: Give the spelling word. Read the sentence. Repeat the spelling word. After all the spelling words are given, reread the words so that students can check their spelling.

Scoring: Score one point for each correct spelling word. Have students enter their scores on the **Student Record.**

"The Marble Champ"
1. We entered the poster *contest*.
2. They *protest* her unfairness.
3. The *target* is an apple.
4. I like the blue glass *marble*.
5. Does the price *include* tax?
6. It is wrong to *exclude* people.
7. We could not *budge* the carton.
8. My family lives on a *budget*.
9. We heard the *blast* from here.
10. The book had a *plastic* cover.
11. He is the spelling *champion*.
12. We finished the *example* in class.
13. They'll never *figure* it out.
14. I bought the *regular* size.
15. The winner gets a *trophy*.

"Breaker's Bridge"
1. We travel *whenever* we can.
2. She does *whatever* they say.
3. That is one *possibility*.
4. It is *impossible* to do.
5. The dogs *guard* their owner.
6. He was the cave's *guardian*.
7. You *crouch* to play marbles.
8. A kangaroo has a *pouch*.
9. The tiny *object* grew larger.
10. They helped with the *project*.
11. Will you *grind* the pepper?
12. Did you *remind* your friends?
13. I do not *recall* the answer.
14. I will *refresh* your soda.
15. Is there an *ache* in your leg?

How It Feels to Fight for Your Life

1. Do you ever watch that *program?*
2. We made *progress* in school.
3. He felt *pressure* to succeed.
4. The radio announced the *emergency.*
5. Her *urgent* phone calls worried me.
6. Do you *suppose* she heard you?
7. I do not *propose* to walk.
8. What *type* of car do you have?
9. He is a *typical* student.
10. We *collect* money for charity.
11. She has a coin *collection.*
12. I looked at a *selection* of tapes.
13. He writes *amazing* stories.
14. I do not like that *flavor.*
15. The nurse gave me a *treatment.*

Words Worth Knowing

1. We like to ski in *Vermont.*
2. Portsmouth is in *New Hampshire.*
3. *Maine* is the Pine Tree State.
4. Who settled *Rhode Island?*
5. Plymouth Rock is in *Massachusetts.*
6. Her family moved to *Maryland.*
7. Washington lived in *Virginia.*
8. Where is *West Virginia?*
9. *Kentucky* is the Bluegrass State.
10. My family lives in *Tennessee.*

Tonweya and the Eagles

1. They need *medical* treatment.
2. She always takes her *medicine.*
3. Try to *connect* the dots.
4. You can't make any *connection.*
5. I like your *suggestion.*
6. She called for *attention.*
7. She wore a *royal* crown.
8. We need *protection.*
9. He will *represent* our class.
10. They *present* prizes to us.
11. She went in that *direction.*
12. We voted in the *election.*
13. Everyone moved *forward.*
14. His *title* was secretary.
15. Our cat is a *different* color.

Review

1. My compass tells *direction.*
2. I got a *different* answer.
3. This *medicine* cures the flu.
4. The party was my *suggestion.*
5. We had an *emergency.*
6. Was *Massachusetts* a colony?
7. Do you *suppose* he'll arrive?
8. This state is *Virginia.*
9. My knees *ache* at night.
10. Feel the *blast* of cold air.
11. We cannot do the *impossible.*
12. I visit *Kentucky* often.
13. Did they ever *figure* it out?
14. That boxer is the *champion.*
15. I can't *connect* these pieces.

Posttest Sentences

When to Posttest: After students have completed work on each word list you use to accompany this unit, use the appropriate group of sentences below to administer the posttest. After students self-correct their posttests, have them record in their **Journals** or on their **Personal Spelling Lists** the words they misspelled.

Directions for Posttesting: Give the spelling word. Read the sentence. Repeat the spelling word. After the spelling words are given, reread the words so that students can check their spelling.

Scoring: Score one point for each correct spelling word. Have students enter their scores on the **Student Record**.

"The Marble Champ"
1. This is a *contest* for skaters.
2. We *protest* high prices.
3. I was shooting at a *target*.
4. She shot her *marble* carefully.
5. Let's *include* your cousin.
6. Why do they *exclude* children?
7. My brother will not *budge*.
8. The *budget* includes food money.
9. The *blast* wrecked the factory.
10. They make *plastic* flowers.
11. The *champion* won easily.
12. Can you explain this *example*?
13. They *figure* out who's next.
14. He is our *regular* coach.
15. We won the largest *trophy*.

"Breaker's Bridge"
1. I'm ready *whenever* you are.
2. I buy her *whatever* she wants.
3. That *possibility* scares me.
4. That is utterly *impossible*.
5. Dragons *guard* the castle.
6. Who is the child's *guardian*?
7. We *crouch* behind the bushes.
8. What is that *pouch*?
9. The *object* was a flying ship.
10. My *project* won first prize.
11. Cooks *grind* many spices.
12. *Remind* me of the date again.
13. I do not *recall* the answer.
14. I will *refresh* myself.
15. I felt an *ache* in my tooth.

How It Feels to Fight
for Your Life

1. The *program* was about nature.
2. Her *progress* is average.
3. The steam *pressure* built up.
4. What do you do in an *emergency?*
5. I got several *urgent* letters.
6. I *suppose* they liked her.
7. They *propose* to build a highway.
8. What *type* of blood do you have?
9. We live in a *typical* town.
10. They *collect* old post cards.
11. We have trash *collection* today.
12. She played a *selection* by Sousa.
13. I had an *amazing* experience!
14. What *flavor* did you choose?
15. The doctor chose this *treatment*.

Words Worth Knowing

1. Maple syrup comes from *Vermont*.
2. I love *New Hampshire*.
3. Augusta is the capital of *Maine*.
4. The Ocean State is *Rhode Island*.
5. Cape Cod is in *Massachusetts*.
6. The song was written about *Maryland*.
7. Richmond is in *Virginia*.
8. *West Virginia* has mountains.
9. Frankfort is in *Kentucky*.
10. The Volunteer State is *Tennessee*.

Tonweya and the Eagles

1. She went to *medical* school.
2. The doctor gave me *medicine*.
3. Can you *connect* my phone?
4. I feel a *connection* to them.
5. That was her *suggestion*.
6. Don't pay *attention* to them.
7. We admired the *royal* jewels.
8. They gave *protection* to the king.
9. Those lines *represent* roads.
10. Please *present* our gift.
11. In which *direction* did he go?
12. He ran in the last *election*.
13. I look *forward* to the party.
14. This book needs a *title*.
15. They like *different* food.

Review

1. We went in that *direction*.
2. Let's travel a *different* way.
3. Aspirin is a kind of *medicine*.
4. Will they take my *suggestion?*
5. The fire created an *emergency*.
6. I love Boston, *Massachusetts*.
7. We *suppose* he got home safely.
8. I went to *Virginia* Beach.
9. I *ache* in every muscle.
10. A *blast* of air opened the door
11. It is *impossible* for me to do.
12. The horse farm is in *Kentucky*.
13. He can't *figure* it out.
14. The *champion* won a prize.
15. She will *connect* your phone.

GETTING TO KNOW YOU

The Best Bad Thing
strawberry*
raspberry
cantaloupe
cucumber*
watermelon
discuss
discussion
chiefly
handkerchief*
scarf
bargain
barge
rascal*
brute
coward

A Wave in Her Pocket
festival
carnival*
tropical
coral
midnight*
twilight
sunrise
sunset
banquet
bouquet
croquet
quiet
Caribbean
seashore
favorite*

Dear Mr. Henshaw
editor
edition
library
librarian*
describe
description*
repel
repulsive
terrified
terrific
typewriter*
diary*
journal
novel
character*

Words Worth Knowing
Ohio
Indiana
Illinois
Wisconsin
Michigan
Mississippi
Louisiana
Arkansas
Missouri
Iowa

Ben and Me
secret
secretary*
scarce*
bare
major
minor*
splendid*
stupid*
cellar*
collar
dollar
beggar
church*
curve
nurse

Review
scarf
journal
novel
Illinois
croquet
Caribbean
festival
tropical
Louisiana
diary
Arkansas
editor
chiefly
banquet
discuss

Pretest Sentences

When to Pretest: Before you introduce each word list you choose to use to accompany this unit, use the appropriate group of sentences below to administer a pretest for the spelling words on that list. After students self-correct their pretests, assign one of the spelling activities provided for practice with spelling strategies.

Directions for Pretesting: Give the spelling word. Read the sentence. Repeat the spelling word. After all the spelling words are given, reread the words so that students can check their spelling.

Scoring: Score one point for each correct spelling word. Have students enter their scores on the **Student Record.**

The Best Bad Thing
1. She ate a *strawberry.*
2. They picked a *raspberry.*
3. My dad planted a *cantaloupe* seed.
4. Would you like a *cucumber?*
5. The *watermelon* tasted good.
6. I won't *discuss* it with you.
7. We had a great *discussion.*
8. We talked *chiefly* about me.
9. I have a white *handkerchief.*
10. Is your *scarf* blue?
11. I made a good *bargain* with him.
12. Don't just *barge* right in.
13. That puppy is a *rascal.*
14. The *brute* beat his dog.
15. The *coward* ran in fear.

Dear Mr. Henshaw
1. An *editor* corrects manuscripts.
2. That is a limited *edition.*
3. I will go to the *library.*
4. I asked the *librarian* for help.
5. Can you *describe* the wallet?
6. Her *description* of me was fine.
7. We need to *repel* that insect.
8. That was a *repulsive* story.
9. The dog was *terrified.*
10. What a *terrific* surprise.
11. I write at my *typewriter.*
12. Don't read my *diary.*
13. Do you keep a *journal?*
14. I read a great *novel.*
15. The *character* was outstanding.

Ben and Me

1. Never tell your *secret*.
2. He hired a *secretary*.
3. Water is *scarce* in the desert.
4. The walls were *bare*.
5. She gave a *major* speech.
6. A cold is a *minor* illness.
7. We had a *splendid* trip.
8. That was a *stupid* idea.
9. Our *cellar* is dark and cool.
10. The coat had a fur *collar*.
11. I gave him a *dollar*.
12. The *beggar* was very poor.
13. They were married in a *church*.
14. She slowed down on the *curve*.
15. The doctor hired a *nurse*.

Words Worth Knowing

1. I used to live in *Ohio*.
2. Have you been to *Indiana*?
3. She lived in *Illinois*.
4. I ate some *Wisconsin* cheese.
5. Detroit is in *Michigan*.
6. We crossed the *Mississippi* River.
7. France sold *Louisiana* to us.
8. Is *Arkansas* the Wonder State?
9. They live on the *Missouri* River.
10. Her family lives in *Iowa*.

A Wave in Her Pocket

1. We held a book *festival*.
2. We raised money with a *carnival*.
3. Florida has a *tropical* climate.
4. The bracelet was made of *coral*.
5. There is no sun at *midnight*.
6. It was gloomy at *twilight*.
7. We watched the *sunrise* together.
8. They worked until *sunset*.
9. We had a huge *banquet*.
10. Do you have the *bouquet*?
11. Have you played *croquet*?
12. Please be very *quiet*.
13. We cruised the *Caribbean*.
14. We played along the *seashore*.
15. That was my *favorite* movie.

Review

1. This *scarf* is itchy.
2. I keep a daily *journal*.
3. This is a very long *novel*.
4. I visited *Illinois*.
5. I put the *croquet* set away.
6. The *Caribbean* Sea is lovely.
7. The *festival* was a lot of fun.
8. I drank a *tropical* punch.
9. New Orleans is in *Louisiana*.
10. Did she keep a *diary*?
11. What is the capital of *Arkansas*?
12. He is a newspaper *editor*.
13. It was *chiefly* about her.
14. Did you attend the *banquet*?
15. I will not *discuss* it.

Posttest Sentences

When to Posttest: After students have completed work on each word list you use to accompany this unit, use the appropriate group of sentences below to administer the posttest. After students self-correct their posttests, have them record in their **Journals** or on their **Personal Spelling Lists** the words they misspelled.

Directions for Posttesting: Give the spelling word. Read the sentence. Repeat the spelling word. After the spelling words are given, reread the words so that students can check their spelling.

Scoring: Score one point for each correct spelling word. Have students enter their scores on the **Student Record.**

The Best Bad Thing
1. Please eat another *strawberry.*
2. I ate the last *raspberry.*
3. My dad ate a *cantaloupe.*
4. I would like a *cucumber.*
5. The *watermelon* was ripe.
6. I won't *discuss* it at all.
7. We had a long *discussion.*
8. They spoke *chiefly* about him.
9. I have a blue *handkerchief.*
10. Is your *scarf* red?
11. I made a bad *bargain.*
12. He will just *barge* in.
13. That kitten is a *rascal.*
14. The *brute* bullied children.
15. The *coward* cried for help.

Dear Mr. Henshaw
1. An *editor* helped the writer.
2. Is that a limited *edition?*
3. I will meet you at the *library.*
4. I told the *librarian* goodbye.
5. He can *describe* the purse.
6. Her *description* was good.
7. We need to *repel* that dog.
8. That was a *repulsive* joke.
9. The cat was *terrified.*
10. What a *terrific* idea.
11. I broke my *typewriter.*
12. Don't take my *diary.*
13. I keep a *journal.*
14. She read my *novel.*
15. The *character* was evil.

Ben and Me

1. Did you tell the *secret?*
2. He saw a *secretary.*
3. Food is *scarce* there.
4. The floor was *bare.*
5. That is a *major* issue.
6. English was my *minor.*
7. We had a *splendid* meal.
8. That was a *stupid* move.
9. Our *cellar* is very small.
10. The *collar* was made of lace.
11. She gave me a *dollar.*
12. The *beggar* was very sad.
13. They were seated in a *church.*
14. There was a *curve* in the road.
15. The *nurse* made a discovery.

Words Worth Knowing

1. I visited in *Ohio.*
2. She lives in *Indiana.*
3. She toured downstate *Illinois.*
4. I drank some *Wisconsin* milk.
5. Lansing is in *Michigan.*
6. We viewed the *Mississippi* River.
7. Baton Rouge is in *Louisiana.*
8. Is *Arkansas* home to you?
9. They explored the *Missouri* River.
10. Her aunt lives in *Iowa.*

A Wave in Her Pocket

1. We held a food *festival.*
2. We enjoyed the music *carnival.*
3. The state is a *tropical* one.
4. The *coral* reef was lovely.
5. He called at *midnight.*
6. It was soon *twilight.*
7. We saw the *sunrise* today.
8. They watched the *sunset.*
9. We had a nice *banquet.*
10. I bought a big *bouquet.*
11. Have you seen the *croquet* set?
12. He was very *quiet.*
13. We sailed the *Caribbean.*
14. We strolled along the *seashore.*
15. That was my *favorite* book.

Review

1. I brought a red *scarf.*
2. She showed me her *journal.*
3. I finished my *novel* yesterday.
4. I came from *Illinois.*
5. I put the *croquet* mallet down.
6. A *Caribbean* island is nice.
7. The *festival* was over too soon.
8. I ate a *tropical* fruit.
9. I love *Louisiana.*
10. Did he take the *diary?*
11. What is a city in *Arkansas?*
12. He is an *editor.*
13. It was *chiefly* about the dog.
14. Did you see the *banquet?*
15. She will not *discuss* it.

WAY TO GO

Klondike Fever
grasp*
clasp
harsh*
marsh
laundry*
pause*
applause
prepared*
comparing
comparison
bicycle*
motorcycle
bacon*
dozen*
quarter*

The Incredible Journey
loyalty
bravery
anxious
anxiety
frantically
rapidly
endure
endurance
survive
revival
vivid
thrive
strain
yield
surrender

The House of Dies Drear
alert*
cautious
careful*
dreadful
harmful
skillful
waffle
shuffle
strangle
fumble*
scramble*
wiggle
smother*
scurry
quiver

Words Worth Knowing
North Carolina
South Carolina
Georgia
Florida
Alabama
North Dakota
South Dakota
Nebraska
Kansas
Colorado

Long Claws
rifle*
pistol
barrel*
cannon
missile
tremble*
stumble
moan*
groan*
growl*
snarl
quake
stagger*
collapse*
screech

Review
endure
survive
yield
Colorado
rifle
pistol
cannon
missile
splendid
Nebraska
major
secret
harmful
waffle
Alabama

Pretest Sentences

When to Pretest: Before you introduce each word list you choose to use to accompany this unit, use the appropriate group of sentences below to administer a pretest for the spelling words on that list. After students self-correct their pretests, assign one of the spelling activities provided for practice with spelling strategies.

Directions for Pretesting: Give the spelling word. Read the sentence. Repeat the spelling word. After all the spelling words are given, reread the words so that students can check their spelling.

Scoring: Score one point for each correct spelling word. Have students enter their scores on the **Student Record.**

Klondike Fever
1. He had a *grasp* of the subject.
2. The *clasp* was broken.
3. It was a *harsh* winter.
4. The *marsh* was filled with birds.
5. Do the *laundry,* please.
6. Please *pause* for breath.
7. The *applause* was deafening.
8. He *prepared* a drink.
9. Are you *comparing* grades?
10. That was a good *comparison.*
11. I rode my *bicycle* home.
12. Do you own a *motorcycle?*
13. The *bacon* was good.
14. I have a *dozen* roses.
15. Give me a *quarter.*

The House of Dies Drear
1. Mice are *alert* to danger.
2. She gave *cautious* advice.
3. He is a *careful* worker.
4. We heard a *dreadful* scream.
5. Is that a *harmful* substance?
6. She was a *skillful* player.
7. I bought a *waffle* iron.
8. Will you *shuffle* the cards?
9. He wanted to *strangle* her.
10. Did she *fumble* with the key?
11. We all *scramble* for cover.
12. I can't *wiggle* my finger.
13. Can you *smother* the sound?
14. I watched the animals *scurry.*
15. Fear made us *quiver.*

Long Claws

1. The pioneer had a *rifle.*
2. He fired the *pistol* into the air.
3. The gun *barrel* was dark metal.
4. There is a *cannon* in our park.
5. The army fired the *missile.*
6. Houses *tremble* in an earthquake.
7. They *stumble* over their toys.
8. Injured people *moan* with pain.
9. The steps *groan* under me.
10. Those dogs *growl* at me.
11. The lions *snarl* at hunters.
12. Explosions made the ground *quake.*
13. The heavy load made me *stagger.*
14. They *collapse* after their race.
15. What was that awful *screech?*

Words Worth Knowing

1. Asheville is in *North Carolina.*
2. Will you visit *South Carolina?*
3. The peaches come from *Georgia.*
4. I toured *Florida* last year.
5. What is the capital of *Alabama?*
6. It's cold in *North Dakota.*
7. Is *South Dakota* cold, too?
8. He is the governor of *Nebraska.*
9. She lives in *Kansas.*
10. I went down the *Colorado* River.

The Incredible Journey

1. We feel great *loyalty* to her.
2. We wrote about her *bravery.*
3. We were *anxious* about it.
4. I noticed his *anxiety.*
5. He looked *frantically* for it.
6. The runner raced *rapidly* away.
7. He will *endure* much pain.
8. This is an *endurance* test.
9. How did the animal *survive?*
10. That play is a *revival.*
11. He likes *vivid* colors.
12. Roses *thrive* in this soil.
13. The horse felt the *strain.*
14. The knights *yield* to the king.
15. They won't *surrender* the town.

Review

1. I can't *endure* hot weather.
2. Wolves *survive* in the woods.
3. Cars should *yield* to bikes.
4. I love the state of *Colorado.*
5. Davy Crockett had a *rifle.*
6. The man carried a *pistol.*
7. We fired a *cannon.*
8. The *missile* shot into space.
9. They lived in a *splendid* home.
10. Do you live in *Nebraska?*
11. They had *major* disagreements.
12. I never tell a *secret.*
13. She tells *harmful* stories.
14. May I have a *waffle?*
15. I visited *Alabama.*

Posttest Sentences

When to Posttest: After students have completed work on each word list you use to accompany this unit, use the appropriate group of sentences below to administer the posttest. After students self-correct their posttests, have them record in their **Journals** or on their **Personal Spelling Lists** the words they misspelled.

Directions for Posttesting: Give the spelling word. Read the sentence. Repeat the spelling word. After the spelling words are given, reread the words so that students can check their spelling.

Scoring: Score one point for each correct spelling word. Have students enter their scores on the **Student Record.**

Klondike Fever

1. He had a *grasp* of mathematics.
2. The *clasp* was silver.
3. It was a *harsh* story.
4. The *marsh* was dark and eerie.
5. I did the *laundry.*
6. Please do not *pause.*
7. There was no *applause.*
8. He *prepared* a speech.
9. Are you *comparing* notes?
10. That was no *comparison.*
11. I rode my *bicycle* today.
12. I own a *motorcycle.*
13. The *bacon* was crisp.
14. I have a *dozen* glasses.
15. She found a *quarter.*

The House of Dies Drear

1. The army was put on *alert.*
2. He is *cautious.*
3. They are *careful* workers.
4. What a *dreadful* shock.
5. That is a *harmful* substance.
6. He is a *skillful* violinist.
7. I bought a *waffle* for brunch.
8. Did you *shuffle* the deck?
9. Did he *strangle* her?
10. He will *fumble* the pass.
11. We all *scramble* for tickets.
12. I can't *wiggle* my toe.
13. Can you *smother* the noise?
14. I watched the mice *scurry.*
15. The cold made us *quiver.*

Long Claws

1. He fired the *rifle.*
2. He put the *pistol* away.
3. The gun *barrel* was rusty.
4. There is a *cannon* on the green.
5. The *missile* was launched.
6. You will *tremble* at the noise.
7. They *stumble* on the curb.
8. I heard such a *moan.*
9. The steps *groan* under his weight.
10. Did the dogs *growl* at you?
11. The cats *snarl* at hunters.
12. We *quake* with fear.
13. The idea will *stagger* you.
14. Did the bridge *collapse?*
15. I heard such a *screech!*

Words Worth Knowing

1. The town is in *North Carolina.*
2. Will you see *South Carolina?*
3. The family comes from *Georgia.*
4. Is Tampa in *Florida?*
5. Dothan is in *Alabama.*
6. I have never been to *North Dakota.*
7. Is *South Dakota* nice?
8. She lives in *Nebraska.*
9. Topeka is in *Kansas.*
10. I saw the *Colorado* Rockies.

The Incredible Journey

1. He demands *loyalty.*
2. Her *bravery* was extraordinary.
3. He was *anxious* about it.
4. I saw his *anxiety.*
5. He looked *frantically* about.
6. The girl raced *rapidly* away.
7. She will *endure* much pain.
8. Is this an *endurance* test?
9. How did the seals *survive?*
10. That song is a *revival.*
11. She paints *vivid* portraits.
12. Roses *thrive* here.
13. The player felt the *strain.*
14. The teams *yield* to the umpire.
15. They won't *surrender* the fort.

Review

1. I can't *endure* it any more.
2. Bears *survive* in the woods.
3. We should *yield* to bikes.
4. I enjoy visiting *Colorado.*
5. Do you have a *rifle?*
6. The man fired a *pistol.*
7. We inspected the *cannon.*
8. The *missile* was launched.
9. They gave a *splendid* party.
10. Do you like *Nebraska?*
11. They had *major* problems.
12. I don't know a *secret.*
13. That was a *harmful* statement.
14. I want a *waffle.*
15. Is *Alabama* a southern state?

Word Lists for Unit 6:

Are You Sure?

How to Think Like a Scientist
experiment*
assignment*
investigation
investigate
scientist*
scientific
ignore*
ignorant
deny
denial
trial
rely
reliable*
accurate
problem*

Willie Bea and the Time the Martians Landed
invade
invasion*
monster*
monstrous
convince*
persuade
persuasion
argue
argument
alien*
Martian
holler*
bellow
bawl
yowl

The News About Dinosaurs
dinosaur*
mammoth
fossil*
skeleton*
skull
remains
sword*
swagger
dagger
preserve*
reserve
restore
reveal
museum*
display

Words Worth Knowing
Nevada
Montana
Minnesota
Wyoming
Utah
Idaho
Oregon
Washington
Hawaii
Alaska

The Incredible Shrinking Machine
schedule*
scheme
active
activity*
atom*
atomic
puzzle*
puzzling
mystery
mysterious
dessert*
desert
commit
committee*
gravity*

Review
persuasion
invade
Minnesota
argue
atom
mystery
Alaska
puzzle
skeleton
skull
sword
museum
problem
Hawaii
scientist

When to Pretest: Before you introduce each word list you choose to use to accompany this unit, use the appropriate group of sentences below to administer a pretest for the spelling words on that list. After students self-correct their pretests, assign one of the spelling activities provided for practice with spelling strategies.

Directions for Pretesting: Give the spelling word. Read the sentence. Repeat the spelling word. After all the spelling words are given, reread the words so that students can check their spelling.

Scoring: Score one point for each correct spelling word. Have students enter their scores on the **Student Record.**

How to Think Like a Scientist
1. We finished the *experiment.*
2. I did the *assignment.*
3. He began the *investigation.*
4. Did you *investigate* the noise?
5. She is a well-known *scientist.*
6. The *scientific* method is well known.
7. Please don't *ignore* me.
8. He was *ignorant* of the decision.
9. You can't *deny* the facts.
10. That *denial* is not strong.
11. The *trial* occurred yesterday.
12. I *rely* on your judgment.
13. Is that *reliable* information?
14. The facts are *accurate.*
15. I can handle any *problem.*

The News About Dinosaurs
1. A *dinosaur* was huge.
2. A *mammoth* is amazing.
3. The explorer found a *fossil.*
4. We saw a human *skeleton.*
5. Are there bones in your *skull?*
6. We buried the animal *remains.*
7. The *sword* was heavy.
8. Look at that *swagger.*
9. The jeweled *dagger* was costly.
10. Please *preserve* the past.
11. Will you *reserve* a seat?
12. They *restore* old houses.
13. The judges *reveal* names.
14. Our *museum* is outstanding.
15. They *display* old jewelry.

The Incredible Shrinking Machine

1. His busy *schedule* is insane.
2. That *scheme* was interesting.
3. She owns *active* wear.
4. That *activity* is strenuous.
5. He split the *atom*.
6. That is an *atomic* reactor.
7. The *puzzle* was challenging.
8. It is *puzzling* to me.
9. That *mystery* will never be solved.
10. Is it *mysterious* or not?
11. She served a rich *dessert*.
12. The Mojave is a large *desert*.
13. I cannot *commit* to that.
14. Is the *committee* elected?
15. *Gravity* is a scientific fact.

Words Worth Knowing

1. Is *Nevada* home?
2. I have visited *Montana*.
3. Is *Minnesota* cold in winter?
4. I know *Wyoming* is in the West.
5. Carol lives in *Utah*.
6. I have never been to *Idaho*.
7. Salem is in *Oregon*.
8. Is *Washington* on the Pacific coast?
9. There are volcanoes in *Hawaii*.
10. The pipeline is in *Alaska*.

Willie Bea and the Time the Martians Landed

1. Did you *invade* the desert?
2. The *invasion* is over.
3. I do not see a *monster*.
4. That was *monstrous*.
5. You can *convince* me.
6. They *persuade* the others.
7. Is *persuasion* powerful?
8. I *argue* with her all the time.
9. The *argument* was over quickly.
10. That was not an *alien*.
11. The movie was about a *Martian*.
12. Did you *holler* at me?
13. The singer can *bellow*.
14. The calves *bawl* in the morning.
15. The baby gave quite a *yowl*.

Review

1. I practiced my powers of *persuasion*.
2. He will *invade* the kingdom.
3. I have a friend in *Minnesota*.
4. They never *argue* with me.
5. When did they split an *atom*?
6. The book was a *mystery*.
7. I want to visit *Alaska*.
8. I finished the *puzzle*.
9. They dug up a *skeleton*.
10. The *skull* was small.
11. She used a silver *sword*.
12. This is a crafts *museum*.
13. I had a *problem* with her.
14. She's going to *Hawaii*.
15. I will become a *scientist*.

Posttest Sentences

When to Posttest: After students have completed work on each word list you use to accompany this unit, use the appropriate group of sentences below to administer the posttest. After students self-correct their posttests, have them record in their **Journals** or on their **Personal Spelling Lists** the words they misspelled.

Directions for Posttesting: Give the spelling word. Read the sentence. Repeat the spelling word. After the spelling words are given, reread the words so that students can check their spelling.

Scoring: Score one point for each correct spelling word. Have students enter their scores on the **Student Record.**

How to Think Like a Scientist
1. We did the *experiment.*
2. I finished the *assignment.*
3. He started the *investigation.*
4. Did you *investigate* the problem?
5. She is a famous *scientist.*
6. We use the *scientific* method.
7. Please don't *ignore* that issue.
8. Are you *ignorant* of it?
9. Don't *deny* the facts.
10. She made a strong *denial.*
11. They went to *trial* yesterday.
12. I *rely* on you totally.
13. Is that source *reliable?*
14. The facts must be *accurate.*
15. I can solve any *problem.*

The News About Dinosaurs
1. A *dinosaur* was a reptile.
2. A *mammoth* was an elephant.
3. The scientist found a *fossil.*
4. We used a human *skeleton.*
5. There are bones in your *skull.*
6. We dug up the animal *remains.*
7. She fought with a *sword.*
8. He had quite a *swagger.*
9. He used a jeweled *dagger.*
10. We want to *preserve* the past.
11. Will you *reserve* a space for us?
12. They *restore* old clothing.
13. The judges *reveal* the winner.
14. Our town has a *museum.*
15. They *display* old coins.

The Incredible Shrinking Machine

1. He has a busy *schedule*.
2. That was a clever *scheme*.
3. She is very *active*.
4. I like that *activity* very much.
5. We studied the *atom* in school.
6. That is the theory of *atomic* fusion.
7. We put the *puzzle* together.
8. It is a *puzzling* theory.
9. That is a *mystery* of science.
10. Is it *mysterious* to you?
11. She fixed a fabulous *dessert*.
12. The Sahara is a large *desert*.
13. I cannot *commit* to that.
14. Are you on the *committee*?
15. *Gravity* makes us circle the sun.

Words Worth Knowing

1. Is *Nevada* the Silver State?
2. I have never toured *Montana*.
3. Is *Minnesota* north of here?
4. I hear *Wyoming* is gorgeous.
5. Bill lives in *Utah*.
6. Potatoes grow in *Idaho*.
7. Portland is in *Oregon*.
8. Is *Washington* near Oregon?
9. Honolulu is in *Hawaii*.
10. Nome is in *Alaska*.

Willie Bea and the Time the Martians Landed

1. Did you *invade* the country?
2. The *invasion* occurred at noon.
3. I saw the *monster*.
4. That was a *monstrous* lie.
5. You cannot *convince* me.
6. They *persuade* others to stay.
7. He is very good at *persuasion*.
8. Don't *argue* with me.
9. They had an *argument*.
10. Was that an *alien*?
11. Watch out for the *Martian*.
12. We *holler* to our friends.
13. The cows can *bellow*.
14. He will *bawl* when frightened.
15. The cat gave quite a *yowl*.

Review

1. The mayor practiced *persuasion*.
2. The Vikings will *invade*.
3. I love *Minnesota*.
4. They always *argue* with me.
5. How do they split an *atom*?
6. The movie was a *mystery*.
7. I know *Alaska* is large.
8. I finish the crossword *puzzle*.
9. They dug up a human *skeleton*.
10. The *skull* had no teeth.
11. She was given a golden *sword*.
12. This is an automobile *museum*.
13. I had a *problem* with my car.
14. Have you been to *Hawaii*?
15. How do you become a *scientist*?

SPELLING ACTIVITIES

The following activities are recommended for students who have progressed from invented or temporary spelling to more conventional spelling.

CREATE YOUR OWN LIST

Encourage students to build personal spelling lists. Invite students to choose up to five words each week to add to the list. These words can be studied and learned along with the program word list. Students may choose words from a particular topic of study or words that they frequently misspell or words that are of special interest to them.

TEST AND RETEST

Use this method to help students gain control of spelling words suitable for their level of spelling knowledge and ability. On the first day of the week, call out the words on the list. Invite students to attempt to spell each one. Then call out the correct spelling of each word. Have students strike through any incorrect spelling and write the correct spelling beside it. You may want to use this activity by having students pair up and call out the words to each other. Encourage students to study the words that they missed for the retest at the end of the week.

If some students spell most of the words on the list correctly the first time, you may want to substitute more words from other sources, such as from their writing or from other subject areas. On the other hand, if a student gets most of the words wrong, and it seems beyond his or her capacity at the moment to learn all of the misspelled words on the list, you may want to substitute words from another list—a list of core words from writing or a lower level list from this program.

PATTERN POWER

Stress the patterns that exist in clusters of words in any given word list. Encourage students to increase their repertoire of words by keeping a section in their spelling notebook that has subsections dedicated to words that fall into various spelling patterns. Students can add to these sections as they wish.

MULTISENSORY STUDY METHOD

Encourage students to study words using these steps:

- Look at the word as your teacher or a friend reads it or says it aloud.
- Say the word aloud to yourself.
- Write the word. Name each letter as you write it.
- Say the word again.
- Check to make sure you spelled the word correctly.
- Cover the word and write it again. Name each letter as you write it.
- Check to make sure you spelled the word correctly. If you did not, erase the word and repeat the two preceding steps.

SPELLING BRAINSTORMS

Choose a word from the weekly list. Invite students to help you spell it. Call on students to offer one letter at a time. Discuss why these letters make sense or do not. Compare the final version with the correct version, and point out any patterns that emerge.

For example, in spelling *gate,* students may offer *gait.* Ask them what has led them to think that this spelling is reasonable, or ask them if they can think of other similar-sounding words that spell the vowel sound *ai.* Then ask if they know of any other words that spell the vowel pattern *a e.* (Note: With beginning spellers this activity will have a different goal. You can invite beginning spellers to listen for the sounds in words and match the letters with the sounds that they hear. You can accept reasonable guesses, even if they are incorrect, because the goal is to encourage the students to use invented or temporary spelling.)

SPELLING INVENTORY

Interview students about spelling. Use some of these questions:

- What is standard spelling?
- Do you think it's important? Why or why not?
- Should you always spell every word correctly in all your writing? Why or why not?
- What do you do when you don't know how to spell a word?
- Do you have any tricks you use to help you to remember how to spell some words?

WORKING WITH GENERALIZATIONS

Have students learn the most useful generalizations. For example—

- Use *i* before *e,* except after *c,* or when it rhymes with *say* as in *neighbor* and *weigh.*
- No English word ends in *v* (except for the slang word *shiv,* meaning knife).
- In words such as *now* and *announce, /ow/* is spelled *ow* at the end of a word, and *ou* in the middle of a word.

Other useful generalizations appear on pages 178-181.

COMMON CONFUSIONS

Have students learn sentences to distinguish commonly confused words. You might want to create a wall poster for them.

"Those two guys went to jail, too."
"We can't accept anyone else except you."
"How will the greenhouse effect affect you?"

WORD SORTS

Word sorts are grouping activities that call students' attention to spelling patterns and other features that words have in common. All word-sort activities use spelling words printed on business-card-sized pieces of tagboard (or cut an index card into three pieces). The words should be within the reading and speaking vocabulary of all the students who participate.

Closed-Ended Word Sort

You can work with two to five students for this activity. Each student has four to eight cards. The words on the cards share a spelling pattern or phonogram (though it helps if a few do not share the same pattern). You or a student leader begins by putting a card on the table. Invite the student on the right to put down any word that he or she has in hand that "goes with" the word on the table. As the student does so, he or she says what the new word has in common with the first word. The next student to the right is then invited to put down any word that she or he has that matches the first two; if the next student is unable to match the first two, he or she can begin a new category. Play continues until all cards are discarded.

This activity can be made more or less structured. With less experienced students, the teacher can prepare the word cards so that almost all of them share the same beginning consonant, or phonogram, or past tense ending, and so on. You may also ask explicitly for words that conform to that pattern.

Independent Word Sort

You can prepare packages of cards that contain words having two, three, or four patterns in common. Individuals or pairs of students may be invited to sort the words into patterns. For follow-up, students can record the words by pattern in a spelling notebook. Further, they may look through books and magazines for other words that have the same spelling patterns, and enter those words in the spelling notebooks, too.

Concentration

You can write a list of spelling words on business-card-sized cards. Number them on the back. Put the cards in a rectangular grid, face down, numbers up. Invite students to take turns turning up pairs of cards. When they find two that arguably share a spelling pattern, they may take them off the table. If winners are desired, students may play in teams; the team with the most cards at the end of the game wins. (Note: With older students, the words may contain the same stem or related morpheme—*tele-, re-, dis-, -graph, bio-*, and so on.)

Word Building

With older students, you can play a variation on the Concentration game. Prepare a set of a dozen words with common stems (*-ology, -graph, -scope, -sphere*, and so on). Number these word cards on the back and place them face down, numbers up, in a rectangular grid. Surround them with prefixes (bound morphemes, such as *tele-, bio-, micro-, geo-*, and so on). Students can take turns turning up word stems in the middle and pairing them with the prefixes around the perimeter.

Daily Edits

Prepare (or better yet, ask a group of students to take turns preparing) a pair of sentences with several of the week's words misspelled in them. Write the sentences on the chalkboard. Ask volunteers to correct the spelling errors.

Rotating Spelling Committee

Before students submit a paper for publication, have them check their spelling with a Spelling Committee. The Spelling Committee should be composed of strong spellers and those who are not as strong. The Committee's job is to look the paper over for words that may be misspelled. The writer's job is to look up in a dictionary any words that are challenged and to correct them before submitting the paper for publication. Students should serve limited terms on the Spelling Committee (two to three weeks).

Shedding Light on Reduced Vowels

Words such as *photograph* have unstressed syllables in which the vowels are reduced and indistinct. Activities can be constructed in which students first mark the doubtful part of a word with a silent or reduced letter, and then think of a related word (or choose one from a list of possibilities) in which the doubtful part is made clear. For a word such as *photograph*, the word *photography* would do. (Other such pairs would be *bomb/bombard; hymn/hymnal; solemn/solemnity; produce/product*.)

Spelling Strategies

One of the most important things every writer does during the proof-reading stage is to check that all of the words in a piece are correctly spelled. Poor spelling is more than an inconvenience to the reader. If even one or two words are spelled incorrectly, your writing may end up meaning something very different from what you wanted to say.

Try spelling difficult words syllable by syllable, saying the word quietly to yourself as you write it. If you pronounce it correctly, your chances of spelling it correctly are improved. Also, try to picture what the word looks like. This will almost always help you to find the correct spelling. Always check your dictionary for any spellings you aren't sure of.

Spelling rules can help you to spell certain kinds of words correctly. Remember—rules are only hints to help you to develop a sense of what's correct and what isn't. English is a tricky language; the following rules almost always have exceptions, so you can't depend on them in every case.

Words with *ie* and *ei*

In most cases, a word is spelled with *ie* for the *e* sound, except when the *e* sound follows the letter *c:*
    chief, belief, yield, niece,
    receive, ceiling, perceive
In most cases, a word is spelled with *ei* when the sound is not *e,* especially if the sound is *a:*
    eight, eighty, freight, neighbor
Be careful, however! These are common exceptions to this rule:
    friend, either, seize, weird

Adding *s* and *es*

In most cases, *s* can be added to a word without any other change in the spelling:
    boy/boys   voice/voices   rock/rocks
If the word ends in *ch, s, sh, x,* or *z,* add *es:*
    bench/benches   dish/dishes   buzz/buzzes
    kiss/kisses   mix/mixes   chorus/choruses
For most nouns ending in a single *f,* change the *f* to *v* and add *es* to form the plural:
    elf/elves   scarf/scarves   loaf/loaves
Here are some exceptions to this rule:
    oaf/oafs   proof/proofs   chief/chiefs

Spelling Strategies and Tips

Most words that end in *ff* simply add *s:*

cliff/cliffs   stuff/stuffs   sniff/sniffs

Words ending in *o*

Most words that end in a vowel followed by *o* add *s* to form the plural:

rodeo/rodeos   folio/folios   studio/studios

Most words that end in a consonant followed by *o* add *es* to form the plural:

hero/heroes   zero/zeroes   potato/potatoes

Some exceptions are words, mostly for musical terms, borrowed from the Italian language. Their plurals are usually formed simply by adding *s:*

piano/pianos   soprano/sopranos   cello/cellos

Sometimes, however, the original Italian plural form is used:

concerto/concerti   libretto/libretti

Adding -es, -ed, -ing, -er, and -est

If a word ends in a consonant followed by *y,* change the *y* to *i* before adding any ending that does not begin with *i:*

ruby/rubies   rely/relies   carry/carried

For most words that end in a vowel followed by *y,* keep the *y* when adding an ending:

enjoy/enjoyed   stray/straying   obey/obeyed

Remember that some irregular verbs ignore this rule to form their past tenses:

say/said   buy/bought   pay/paid

In most cases, if a one-syllable word ends in one vowel and one consonant, the consonant doubles when an ending that begins with a vowel is added:

sag/sagged   trip/tripping   thin/thinnest

For most two-syllable words ending in one vowel and one consonant, the consonant doubles only if the accent falls on the second syllable:

trigger/triggered   bother/bothering

BUT: begin/beginning   prefer/preferred

If a word ends in a silent *e,* drop the *e* when adding an ending that begins with a vowel:

> lose/loser   loose/loosest   shave/shaver
> tape/taped   write/writing   breathe/breathing

Adding prefixes and suffixes

When you add a prefix to a word, the spelling of the base word usually stays the same:

> tie/untie   behave/misbehave   arm/disarm

When you add a suffix, the spelling of the base word may change. If the base word ends in silent *e,* drop the *e* before a suffix that begins with a vowel:

> operate/operator   type/typist   love/lovable

For most words ending in silent *e,* keep the *e* when adding a suffix that begins with a consonant:

> love/loveless   shame/shameful   elope/elopement

When you add the suffix *-ness* or *-ly,* the spelling of the base word usually does not change:

> strange/strangely   fine/fineness   quick/quickly

Common exceptions are adjectives ending in a single consonant following a vowel:

> metric/metrically

Other exceptions are certain one-syllable words ending in two vowels or a vowel and *y:*

> true/truly   due/duly   gay/gaily

If a word ends in *y* and has more than one syllable, change the *y* to *i* before adding *-ness* or *ly:*

> happy/happily/happiness   crazy/crazily/craziness

Spelling Strategies and Tips

Homophones

Homophones—words with different meanings and spellings that sound alike—are responsible for a great many misspellings. Be sure you know the *meaning* of the homophone you want to use. That will usually help you to spell it correctly. Here are a few of those most often misspelled and misused:

rain/rein/reign   pore/pour   sheer/shear
chilly/chili/Chile   flare/flair   bough/bow
pair/pear/pare   forth/fourth   higher/hire
close/clothes   to/too/two   lose/loose
piece/peace/peas   hours/ours   real/reel
through/threw   accept/except   so/sew/sow
stationary/stationery   principal/principle

As we pointed out at the beginning of this section, rules of spelling won't be enough to help you to spell correctly in every case. There are many words in the English language whose spellings seem to obey no rules at all or to contradict the rules you've taken so much trouble to learn. Some of them *do* follow the rules but are tricky to spell anyway. The only way to spell these "problem" words correctly every time is to memorize them.

To help you to do this, we've picked out some of the words that seem to give most people most trouble the most often—the words that you will see most frequently misspelled. Use this list or your dictionary often, whenever you are unsure of a word. The more often you see a word's correct spelling, the more likely you are to remember it for your own future use.

absent	argue	canoe	disappear
accept	argument	caught	disappoint
accident	assistant	certain	disaster
accompany	athlete	challenge	disease
ache		channel	doubt
address	balance	character	drawer
afraid	bathe	chemical	
again	beautiful	chief	early
aisle	because	close	elementary
alley	believe	clothes	elephant
all right	bicycle	color	embarrass
ally	bought	congratulate	encyclopedia
although	breathe	cough	enough
always	brilliant	cousin	especially
ancient	broad	criticize	excellent
angel	brought		except
angle	bruise	daily	
ankle	build	determine	familiar
answer	business	develop	fare
appearance	buy	diamond	February
appetite		different	foreign
appreciate		difficult	forty

fourth	lightning	permanent	similar
friend	liquid	persuade	situation
frighten	loose	pleasant	soldier
furniture	lose	pleasure	sour
		poison	station
genuine	marriage	position	straighten
government	meant	prayer	strategy
graduate	meteor		successful
grammar	minute	quality	sugar
growth	misspell	quiet	sure
guess	money		surprise
guest	mystery	rapid	sword
		realize	
half	national	receive	taught
happiness	necessary	reckless	their
haul	necessity	recognize	they're
heaven	neighbor	recommend	though
height	nickel	relief	thousand
hour	niece	religious	through
	nineteenth	responsible	tired
icicle	ninetieth	restaurant	tomorrow
interest	ninety	review	toward
interrupt	ninth	rhyme	treasure
island	nursery	rhythm	trouble
			truly
judgment	obedient	safety	tying
justice	occasion	schedule	
	official	school	variety
knelt	often	scissors	
knowledge	once	scratch	waffle
	onion	secretary	weather
label	opportunity	seize	weird
laboratory		separate	we're
language	package	seventh	whether
lawyer	patience	sew	
library	pear	shepherd	you're
license	people	silence	

Spelling Forms

WORDS OF MY OWN

When you proofread your writing, keep track of the words that you have trouble spelling. Note those words in the **Quick-Check Box**. You can also jot down any other words that are of particular interest to you in the **Quick-Check Box**. You can then double-check your words in the dictionary and add them to the list below.

┌─ Quick-Check Box ───┐
│   │
│   │
│   │
│   │
│   │
└──┘

Ask a friend to hear you spell your Personal Spelling List words aloud. Ask your friend to mark with a ✓ the words you spelled correctly.

☐ _____   ☐ _____
☐ _____   ☐ _____
☐ _____   ☐ _____
☐ _____   ☐ _____
☐ _____   ☐ _____
☐ _____   ☐ _____
☐ _____   ☐ _____
☐ _____   ☐ _____
☐ _____   ☐ _____
☐ _____   ☐ _____
☐ _____   ☐ _____
☐ _____   ☐ _____
☐ _____   ☐ _____
☐ _____   ☐ _____
☐ _____   ☐ _____
☐ _____   ☐ _____

UNIT 1: UNFORGETTABLE PLACES LEVEL 11

Word List	Pretest Score	Posttest Score	Personal Spelling List
1. *The Wreck of the "Zephyr"*			
2. *The Talking Eggs*			
3. *The Voyage of the "Dawn Treader"*			
4. *Dive to the Coral Reefs*			
5. Words Worth Knowing			
6. Review			

UNIT 2: TRANSFORMATIONS LEVEL 11

Word List	Pretest Score	Posttest Score	Personal Spelling List
1. *New Providence: A Changing Cityscape*			
2. *Be an Inventor*			
3. *The Gold Coin*			
4. *The Shimmershine Queens*			
5. Words Worth Knowing			
6. Review			

UNIT 3: AGAINST THE ODDS LEVEL 11

Word List	Pretest Score	Posttest Score	Personal Spelling List
1. "The Marble Champ"			
2. "Breaker's Bridge"			
3. *How It Feels to Fight for Your Life*			
4. *Tonweya and the Eagles*			
5. Words Worth Knowing			
6. Review			

UNIT 4: GETTING TO KNOW YOU LEVEL 11

Word List	Pretest Score	Posttest Score	Personal Spelling List
1. *The Best Bad Thing*			
2. *Dear Mr. Henshaw*			
3. *Ben and Me*			
4. *A Wave in Her Pocket*			
5. Words Worth Knowing			
6. Review			

UNIT 5: WAY TO GO LEVEL 11

Word List	Pretest Score	Posttest Score	Personal Spelling List
1. "Klondike Fever"			
2. *The House of Dies Drear*			
3. *Long Claws*			
4. *The Incredible Journey*			
5. Words Worth Knowing			
6. Review			

UNIT 6: ARE YOU SURE? LEVEL 11

Word List	Pretest Score	Posttest Score	Personal Spelling List
1. *How to Think Like a Scientist*			
2. *The News About Dinosaurs*			
3. "The Incredible Shrinking Machine"			
4. *Willie Bea and the Time the Martians Landed*			
5. Words Worth Knowing			
6. Review			

Class Record—Pretest

Name	Level_____ Unit_____	Level_____ Unit_____
1.		
2.		
3.		
4.		
5.		
6.		
7.		
8.		
9.		
10.		
11.		
12.		
13.		
14.		
15.		
16.		
17.		
18.		
19.		
20.		
21.		
22.		
23.		
24.		
25.		

Class Record—Posttest

Name	Level_____ Unit_____	Level_____ Unit_____
1.		
2.		
3.		
4.		
5.		
6.		
7.		
8.		
9.		
10.		
11.		
12.		
13.		
14.		
15.		
16.		
17.		
18.		
19.		
20.		
21.		
22.		
23.		
24.		
25.		

Cumulative Word List

Cumulative Word List   Level 11

accurate
ache
active
activity
adventure
advertisement
Alabama
Alaska
alert
alien
allow
amazing
ancient
anxiety
anxious
apartment
applause
arch
architect
argue
argument
Arizona
Arkansas
assignment
atom
atomic
attention

bacon
banquet
bare
bargain
barge
barrel
bawl
beggar
bellow

bicycle
blast
border
bouquet
bravery
bruise
brute
budge
budget

California
Canada
cannon
cantaloupe
capital
capitol
careful
Caribbean
carnival
cautious
celebrate
celebration
cellar
champion
character
chiefly
church
clasp
collapse
collar
collect
collection
Colorado
commit
committee
comparing
comparison

condition
connect
Connecticut
connection
constant
contest
convince
coral
coward
create
creative
croquet
crouch
cruise
cucumber
cupboard
curve
cushion

dagger
defeat
Delaware
delicious
denial
deny
deposit
describe
description
desert
dessert
diary
different
dinosaur
direction
discover
discuss
discussion

display
distant
disturb
dollar
dozen
dreadful

edition
editor
election
emergency
emptiness
endurance
endure
England
enormous
entertain
even
evening
example
exclude
expect
experiment
explore

fail
favorite
festival
figure
final
flavor
Florida
fold
folk tale
fortunate
fortune
forward

fossil
France
frantically
freedom
fumble
furnace
furniture

Georgia
govern
government
grasp
gravity
grind
groan
growl
guard
guardian
guess
guide
guilt
guitar

handkerchief
harmful
harsh
Hawaii
holler

Idaho
ignorant
ignore
Illinois
image
imagine
imitate
imitation

impossible
include
Indiana
inform
information
inscription
inspect
instant
invade
invasion
invent
invention
investigate
investigation
Iowa
iron

Jamaica
Japan
jewel
journal

Kansas
Kentucky

laundry
legend
librarian
library
local
location
Louisiana
loyalty

Maine
major
mammoth

manage
marble
marsh
Martian
Maryland
Massachusetts
medical
medicine
mention
Mexico
Michigan
midnight
Minnesota
minor
missile
Mississippi
Missouri
mixture
moan
modern
monster
monstrous
Montana
motorcycle
movement
museum
mutter
mysterious
mystery

narrow
Nebraska
neither
Nevada
New Hampshire
New Jersey
New Mexico

New York
North Carolina
North Dakota
notice
noticeable
novel
nurse

object
Ohio
Oklahoma
operation
opposite
order
Oregon

palace
pale
pause
Pennsylvania
perform
performance
persuade
persuasion
pistol
plastic
pleasant
pleasure
port
position
possibility
pouch
powerful
precious
prepared
present
preserve

pressure
private
problem
produce
program
progress
project
propose
protection
protest
prove
Puerto Rico
puzzle
puzzling

quake
quarter
quiet
quiver

rapidly
rascal
raspberry
recall
recover
reduce
refresh
regular
reliable
rely
remains
remind
repel
represent
repulsive
reserve
respect

restore
return
reveal
revival
Rhode Island
rifle
rise
royal
Russia

sailor
scarce
scarf
schedule
scheme
scientific
scientist
scold
scramble
screech
scurry
seashore
secret
secretary
selection
shepherd
shiver
shriveled
shuffle
skeleton
skillful
skull
smother
snarl
sneaking
sort
South Carolina

South Dakota
Spain
sparrow
special
splendid
sputter
stagger
stomach
strain
strangle
strawberry
stumble
stupid
suggestion
sunrise
sunset
suppose
surface
surprise
surrender
survive
swagger
swallow
sword

target
temper
Tennessee
terrific
terrified
Texas
thrive
title
treasure
treatment
tremble
trial

tribal
tribe
trophy
tropic
tropical
turbulent
twilight
twisted
type
typewriter
typical

United States
urgent
Utah

Vermont
Virginia
vivid

waffle
Washington
watermelon
West Virginia
whatever
wheelbarrow
whenever
whimper
whisper
who'd
who's
whose
who've
wiggle
Wisconsin
wise
wonderful

HANDWRITING RESOURCES

HANDWRITING RESOURCES

The handwriting resources included in this section of the **Writer's Workshop** include the following materials:

- Handwriting Reminders and Self-Check Guide
- Handwriting Guidelines
- Alphabet Models

The list of handwriting reminders and self-check questions is intended as an aid for students as they check their written work for legibility. This check is consistently emphasized in the Writing Process lessons during the last stages of the process when students prepare their final copy for sharing.

The handwriting guidelines include models illustrating elements of legibility such as smoothness of stroke, letter shape, letter size, and so on.

Since legibility is crucial for effective communication, a cursive alphabet is provided as an aid to students so that they can compare their own handwriting with standard letter models.

You may want to duplicate and distribute these materials so that students can refer to them throughout the year. A good place for students to keep these materials would be in their writing folders.

Handwriting Reminders

Steps to Follow

1. Sit in a natural, easy way.
2. Sit up straight.
3. Hold your pencil lightly but firmly.
4. Place your paper correctly.

Self-Check Questions

✓ Is my handwriting smooth?
✓ Are my letters evenly spaced?
✓ Are my words evenly spaced?
✓ Are my letters shaped correctly?
✓ Are my letters the correct size?
✓ Do all of my letters sit on the baseline?
✓ Do my capital letters touch the top line?
✓ Do all of my letters slant in the same direction?

Handwriting Guidelines

Smoothness

Make each letter smooth and clear.

My favorite books are mysteries.

Spacing

Space each letter evenly.

I read a book a week.

Shape

Make each letter the correct shape.

Do you like to write stories?

Size

Make each letter the correct size.

Will you let me borrow your book?

ALIGNMENT

Make each letter touch the lines correctly.

I read all that author's books.

SLANT

Make your letters slant in the same direction.

My favorite author is Chris Van Allsburg.

Handwriting Models

Alphabet Models

A B C D E F G H I
J K L M N O P Q R
S T U V W X Y Z

a b c d e f g h i
j k l m n o p q r
s t u v w x y z

A B C D E F G H I
J K L M N O P Q R
S T U V W X Y Z

a b c d e f g h i
j k l m n o p q r
s t u v w x y z